Outside-Inside-Outside

Escaping from Prison

Kent Philpott and Friends

EVM

Earthen Vessel Media, LLC

Outside-Inside-Outside
Escaping from Prison

Published 2026 by Earthen Vessel Media, LLC
San Rafael, CA 94903
www.earthenvesselmedia.com

Current paperback edition ISBN: 978-1-946794-33-8

Library of Congress Control Number: 2026908488

Cover design by Liz Stanley

Book Design by Katie L. C. Philpott

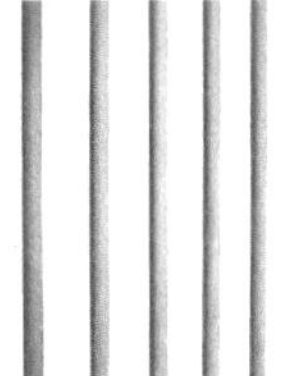

Dedication

Over the course of several years, a number of inmates at San Quentin Prison have contributed to the contents of this book, most of whom played for one of the prison's Giants baseball teams. More than one told me that they were glad to contribute a word or two that might help somebody. So, to these men this book is dedicated.

Thank you Bilal, Chris, Chuck, Curtis, Dave, Doug, Duck, Eli, Frankie, Johnny, Junkyard, Kevin, Louie, Mario, Marcus. Mike, Pete, Terry, and Stafont.

Contents

Preface

This book has three main sections—the Outside-Inside-Outside chapters—and each section is followed by one, two, or three short pieces by a wide variety of people: convicts and friends, as well as cops and correctional officers. There are also a few extra but related pieces. The goal is to draw upon the experience, knowledge, and wisdom of as broad a group as possible to prevent some from going inside in the first place and beyond that to help convicts get outside again and then remain outside.

To encourage a we/they mentality is to promote a way of dealing with life that can only lead to failure. To turn things around it must be seen that it does take the whole "village" to at least slow down the rates of incarceration and recidivism present today. Those who find themselves working somewhere in the criminal justice system care deeply about these things just as much as those who are caught up in the system. Prison is not a cash cow or a for-profit industry, an idea that merely fosters the we/they mind-set and is a backbone of those who war against the powers that be. I have encountered this for thirty years at

San Quentin, especially from those newly imprisoned, and have witnessed what a roadblock it is to living free and productive lives outside.

Many convicts I have encountered and have come to know and like are still in, but I am out, and the reason I am writing this book is to prevent others from going inside in the first place. But if you are inside, there are some ideas on how to get out, and once out, something about how to stay out.

I have never been in except as a volunteer at San Quentin, the last half of which has been as baseball coach for the San Quentin Giants. Sitting in the dugout, patrolling the outfield during batting practice, or visiting guys by going cell to cell, which I did for sixteen years, I picked up some knowledge. Who I am means little except to say that, over the years, I learned something about how people end up in prison, garnered some proven methods on how to get out, and then once out, how to stay out—all of which are rather complicated.

People who are not insiders will say, "Well, he or she made a choice." And I cannot help but think, wow, how very ignorant, how very uninformed about how life really is for a many people.

What about Jerome who grew up in a black ghetto, never knew his father, and was raised by his grandmother until age thirteen, during which time his mother became the State of California. Then, having learned the ways of the street, and seeing he needed to gang up, he became a banger. To get accepted by his homies he had to shoot someone from a rival gang, which he tried to do but missed, and instead put a 9mm slug through a bystander, who fortunately survived. Of course, Jerome was drunk, stoned, and stupid when he laid in wait for his target, and besides that, if he had refused the job, he might have gotten whacked himself.

Then Jose made it all the way from Guatemala, from which he escaped to save his very life, moved in with some relatives in San Jose, and to survive had to become a mule for his gang's drug business. At the advanced age of 17, not able to read or write and unable to speak much English, he got caught with a large cache of dope and will do at least six years. Did he make a choice?

Then Frank, repeatedly raped by his grandfather when he was 8 years old, escaped by finally getting himself arrested, starting a series of "visits" to juvenile facilities and finally the Youth Authority. He picked up a case of HIV at about age 13, got out for a few years, and lived in foster care. Again he got molested and started smoking a lot of dope to put it out of his head. By age 17 he had one strike for burglary—after all, dope doesn't grow on trees—and by age 19 he had picked up two more strikes, all non-violent crimes, all around supporting his need to be stoned out of his mind. I guess he had made a decision, since obviously he passed on a number of great career opportunities.

While the content of this book is aimed mainly at convicts or would-be convicts, my hope is to keep language and top-heavy insider talk to a minimum, so that the book can find its way into more places. At the expense of seeming inauthentic, I am letting the content speak for itself.

All right, I'll stop now, but there are a few hundred more examples that could be expressed here. Sure, there are those who made poor choices who maybe could have done otherwise—perhaps the older convicts who somehow gave up and considered being in prison an acceptable career choice. I mean, locked up in a tiny cell for years at least guarantees a dry place to live, food, and medical attention. Not bad for a whole lot of people.

It is agreed that prisons are necessary institutions. Surprisingly, not everybody who volunteers at prisons are necessarily progressive liberals who think that anarchy is the way to go. Prisons are places for people whom we do not want out among us. That is it: we have to lock some people up, because, due to their tortured and disturbed states of mind, no one is safe around them. The vast majority of the people in prison are there because they need to be, considering the terrible lives they ended up with. Let us understand, then, that I am not protesting the reality of our need for prisons and the awful conditions so many convicts find themselves in.

The intent for this book is to say something that might help somebody stay out of prison, but failing that, provide some ways to find a way out, and once out, stay out.

If you, dear reader, are or were part of the correctional system of any state and wish to contribute to a second edition of this book, please contact me at kentphilpott@comcast.net.

1: Outside Not Inside

Being outside is far better than being inside; this is a superior life goal. We know, however, that some don't really care. This book is for those who want to stay outside, or if inside, want to work to get outside, and if once inside and now outside, want to stay there.

Maybe as youngsters or teen-agers, the idea of spending some time in jail might have seemed cool. Risk taking was in the genes, in the blood, and despite the horror stories, most thought it was possible to get away with whatever behavior seemed suitable for the immediate goal. For sure, few had any idea how radical it really was to get locked-up.

Almost no one realizes that the worst part of jail is being forced to be with some (other) really messed up people. Then there are the cops and the guards, in uniforms and with guns, who often care nothing about what happens to those they have power over. There are the good, the bad, and the really ugly in jails, some of whom are looking for a young kid to sexually molest, and not a quick fondle either. Lock-ups have to do with race, sex, and dope. Cool quickly turns to fear, and fear starts killing from the inside out.

What happens in a lock-up changes us forever, but we can't see what is happening to us. The fact is, we are never the same again. We must take on the persona of bad to survive, even transforming how to see our whole environment. In not many moments in time everything about how we see ourselves, others, and the world changes, and permanently.

Scare tactics rarely work. Scared Straight, a program for at-risk youth, attempted that to a degree. It only works with some, but the neighborhood that encouraged risky behavior says, "So what? I am tough, I can handle it," and these thoughts derail any progress the "do-gooders" attempt. These kids don't wake up to the fact that they are in the process of wasting their lives until it is too late. Our guess is that only those who share our life goal of being outside and staying outside will be reading this, so let us go to work.

We assume that you don't want to end up in jail, whether a youth or adult facility. While everyone's circumstances are different, if you have simply been unable to avoid it, you might want to skip right to chapter two. Whatever is going on, give it a chance. Keep reading.

Friends

This is where it all starts—the people we hang out with. If they are bad news, dangerous people, we are in trouble.

Sometimes there is little choice—we are stuck in a place and time with "friends" we didn't necessarily choose. But it is better to be a loner, look for older more stable people as our friends. They might be found in various parts of the neighborhood. Maybe a church, a school, a sports group. We crave to play some football, basketball, or baseball—and join the team! Even choir, drama club, stamp club, math club, whatever, to learn something new and be with people who live a different kind of life. I am talking a serious choice here.

Getting respect by punching somebody hard, cracking them with a bat, sticking a blade, or firing a shot—any screw-up can do that. Being tough, thinking the girls prefer a bad boy is also a dead-end path, and the girls who admire the bad boys are bad girls, and vice versa, and nothing much good comes from it. If you don't like what I am saying, I hope you don't find out the hard way.

Being a man

What's a man? What really is tough?

When we were kids we thought like kids, so we wanted to show we were tough and not afraid of anything. We would put a big hurt on another kid, from another part of town, in a different gang—and we didn't even know the guy. How completely stupid to ruin our lives to show a bunch of friends we had what it takes. In fact, we were only cowards who were stealing other kid's lives. So much disrespect all around that doesn't cancel out.

One must learn is that respect has to be earned. If you want to be respected as a real banger, then be prepared to spend your youth in prison with old, weird cons who will be glad to see you step off the bus.

Being a man is who you are, not what you do. Anyone can kill someone else by pulling a trigger; all you have to be is drunk, stoned, or loaded, not to mention, stupid. The man who walks away is wise; he may pay the price for that, when stupid tries to tell stupid what to do. A real man stands alone and does not need to hide behind the crowd. A real man can stand being rejected when he refuses to go along to get along. Some very hard choices have to be made, but that is what being a man is all about.

Life is a war

Life is hard from day one. Families can be a disaster for all kinds of reasons, and it makes no sense to wonder why and get mad about it and try to find a way to make somebody pay.

There you are, just a kid, having to figure it all out for yourself, and all you know is what you see all around you. You actually see, hear, and know guys who have been in prison, who have some swagger, some influence, some respect, and the impressionable think going to prison is cool.

Yes, there are so many things to be afraid of, and worrying about what others think of you, that thing called peer-pressure, can be huge. Being afraid of what might happen, if you don't go along with the group, can bring major inner personal conflict. We all want to be liked and respected, but that can earn you some real jail time. It's war, and you are trapped in it.

There are no easy answers here, no five simple steps to overcoming fear and winning the battles. What may be enough is that you understand what you are dealing with and that you are not alone—you are not the only one to have been on the front lines of this war.

You have to be smart to stay outside. You have to fight to stay outside. Take a look at those who went away and see what they lost; check out those who came back, too. Maybe some got "rehabilitated," but most did not; they just got on the treadmill of outside then inside then outside, over and over. This is no way to live. It is war out there, so you have to be tough and fight, even if you have to do it all alone—a one man army.

Keep away from war zones

Where are you most likely to get into serious trouble?

Hanging out at the corner? Or, late night at the club? How about a birthday party where dozens, or even hundreds, show up? Maybe driving around blasting music while juiced?

In the Bay Area newspapers, we often read about a shooting at a club that attracts crowds of kids late at night on the weekends. It's begging for trouble. Yes, you have to find something else to do, something that won't be a ticket to prison. Yes, you will not look cool. Yes, you might miss a good time. But yes, you stand a far better chance of staying outside, and that makes all the difference in the world.

You know how it goes: a few friends invite you along for a little mid-night ride, to be cool, get a little stoned, flashing a weapon or two, cruising where there are likely to be others doing the same, and bang, you are in over your head. Stay home, say no, and don't be shy about it.

It boils down to being smart about how to have fun while not exposing yourself to madness. The stories I could tell! So many wish desperately they had learned to be okay staying at home listening to music, playing cards with a younger brother or sister, doing Facebook, texting, reading a book—anything, anything rather than being out looking for trouble and being cool.

If you hang out in a war zone, don't be shocked if you end up a casualty!

Run from fights

Sometimes you must stand your ground—this is understood. But a lot of times the fight is not worth it.

Pride is often the reason for throwing a punch, pulling a trigger, or stabbing with the blade. Then what? Who is helped? What gain has been made? Who is better off? Usually the answer is—no one. Who now has to pay a large price, in addition to the person that was hurt, or killed, and their family and friends?

If at all possible, run from a fight. Do not even go into the vicinity of a battle ground; and you know where those are. Who cares what others think? You do not want to be captive to what others say or think about you. They can just kiss it off.

A man has to know his limitations, so said Clint Eastwood's character Dirty Harry, and it is no surprise to learn that you are made out of flesh while knives and bullets are made out of steel.

If you have to let go of steam, then play football, wrestle, learn to box, become a runner, get a bike (the kind you pedal), work out and sweat and get really tired.

Needing cash

You see it everywhere—people wearing new clothes just like the people on TV, fast, cool cars all tricked out, iPads, iPhones, and all the rest of the techy stuff, lots of dope to get the girls, but no cash at all and no real prospect of getting any, legally that is.

More basic is money to get food and pay the rent. The social security check grandma gets isn't going very far. Food stamps help, yet the clerk won't let you walk out with any high-octane juice. Face it, life is passing you by and you get deeper into misery every day.

What is the solution? Can't get a job, no money to borrow, no relative or friend better off than you are: might seem like the only thing to do is get a gun and be a bread winner.

The above three paragraphs are a living reality for many; they virtually live without hope of any significant change. It is not surprising they find themselves inside. What hope is there?

Here are some ideas:

One, take any job at all and never mind what anybody else says.

Two, save whatever you can, even if you have to live like a monk in the desert, because staying outside is better than the alternative.

Three, think about joining the military. I did, and it made all the difference.

Four, find some way to be of service where you live like cutting grass, sweeping up stores, walking dogs, scavenging for cans and bottles.

Five, find union halls and sign up for whatever you can, even hire out for free just to learn new skills. Maybe the local high school has training for the trades. Maybe there's a real trade school nearby that gives scholarships.

Six, check out want ads in newspapers and on websites on the internet.

Outside you certainly need cash, but inside you need cash, too, and the ways you will have to get it inside you will mostly not like. We all have that deep desire to have things; we have to live and at least get the basics taken care of, but find a way to make honest cash, and pay taxes, too. Cheaters tend to fall prey to weirdness, which doesn't work in the real world. Ripping people off to satisfy yourself or supplying someone's dope habit is no humanitarian deed. Using people to get what you want will eventually mean having the bars close behind you.

Wanting to be somebody

Do you look up to someone who has done some time? If you do, this is not good, unless they have changed their ways and their attitudes as a result! Plain and simple.

You don't have to look down on ex-cons, but you don't

want to glamorize them either. Television programs and movies do, but these just want to sell you tickets and products. You see a film where people are firing cool looking guns, who have sexy girl friends, and lead exciting lives—on a screen. If you want to be like them, you've been sold, manipulated, and deceived.

Do you really think highly of a thief or a drunk or a stoner or a killer or a mugger or a thug or a gangster? Probably you don't deep down. How about those who have respect on the street for one reason or another—is this guy a hero to you? Do you want to please the bad boys, have them honor you when you do their bidding? If so, get ready to go inside.

Being tough and dangerous, doing violent things, hurting people, robbing people—these may result in being feared in the neighborhood, but it will not earn actual respect. The bad boy may gain a reputation, but others will merely fear and hate him—he is nothing more than a bully and a thug.

Often, sub-cultures within the larger society see criminal activity to be the best way to live, while the rest are considered suckers who deserve to be ripped off. This is the gangster mentality, and within it there is a complex reward system that promotes the outlaw lifestyle. Guys at the top learn how to get underlings to do what they want, which is doing the dirty, illegal, work.

Every week, the news shows have videos of gangs of young people all dressed in black attire with black hoodies and masks running into a store, smashing all the display cases, grabbing everything valuable in sight, and running out of the building, sometimes having seriously hurt store owners or patrons, getting into get-away vehicles, and speeding off in all directions with the loot. The motivation is strong: either you do what you are told to do, including murder, or you are not part of the gang family. And yes, many times you have no choice in a matter. What will happen to a young person who refuses to join in the smash-and-grab gang?

The whole idea of who a "somebody" is needs to be thought through and questioned. Not much of a good deal to spend years behind bars to please "somebody."

If you have a problem, get help

If you have something going—a drug or alcohol problem—get help, because you won't solve it yourself. It's a big mistake to think you are tougher than dope and booze—you aren't, and it is total self-deception to think otherwise.

Your life is hard, brutal, miserable, and overwhelming, so you look for a place to hide. The age old lie. Life is like this for everyone, to one degree or another. Don't think that because a person has a lot of advantages in life—a good family, money, and all the necessities, they are living pain free. No, every critter who lives on the planet struggles. Our culture is loaded with ways out of feeling the trouble, by chemistry that is—this is the way for myriads of people, and it leads quickly to being inside.

You might be saying that you can get almost anything you want inside, but at a price, often a high price. It might be your body, having to give someone your desserts, buy stuff at canteen for them, or lean on outsiders to get contraband inside, and a hundred other things, none of which are a good bargain. To put it another way—you end up being a big loser.

Many have heard of Alcohol or Narcotics Anonymous—good programs—and if drugs, and it doesn't matter which one. If marijuana, booze, even beer are a problem, then get help. It doesn't matter whether the substance is legal, because the makers and distributors of all that don't care what it does to you, only that you want more.

Now suppose you like the stuff that's not legal. Be clear now, you have to buy it, stash it, and defend that stash. You can get set up, ripped off, maybe experience a home invasion by someone who knows you have the stuff. Plus, and worst of all, it puts you in regular contact with people who can be dangerous and even land you in jail. Lots of risks involved including the potential of destroying your life. Not a good trade-off.

In your heart you may not want people to know the trouble you are in, or worse, you don't care if people know. When you have gotten to the point where you do not actually care what happens to you—hell is looking for company. If you have some chemical slowly killing you, you have to be smart and deal with it. It takes more character and courage to admit a problem than not. To stay outside you really have to want to stay outside.

Staying in school

Are you in school? Stay there. Take all the classes you can, show up every day, be on time if not five minutes early, respect the teachers, and do the homework. If you are an athlete, or think you might be, go out for a sport, any sport, especially a team sport. Take trades classes like auto mechanics or machine shop or construction.

School is a great place to make friends, meet girls, or if you are a girl, meet boys, and you can work out that muscle that will do you great good—your brain. Right, your brain is a muscle, and if you don't use it you will lose it. A worn out cliché for sure, but very true nevertheless.

Schools usually have other specialty groups going— band, choir, drama, and lots more. If your friends laugh at you for this, let them be your old friends while you are busy making new ones.

Did I say something disrespectful of your friends? Maybe, but it is just that I want to see you stay outside instead of being inside. It is simple—we all learn to fit in with our friends, and if your friends are up to no good, so will you, almost 100% of the time. Some of the friends are destined for prison. Now you have read this, so now you know. It is up to you.

Let me hit the sports thing a little harder: if at all possible, if there is any interest at all, give sports a try. You don't have to be the number one best player, you might be the worst, but go out for the team. If you don't make it, find another one. Track is a sport that takes almost everyone and anyone, and there are others. Don't give up, don't be intimidated—the worst thing that can happen is you completely fail as a jock. This is not the end of the world and may lead to some other group on campus that may turn out to be a big deal.

Let's say you are lousy at sports, as most are, but then think about playing a musical instrument, which will be a super blessing to you all the rest of your life. Now you are approaching cool—learning about an instrument, learning to read music, maybe even writing music and composing lyrics—almost no end to the fun. You might even get rich and famous! Well maybe not, but the girls will be impressed.

Going to church

What about church? Almost everything said about school can be said for church, since both open new worlds and new opportunities. You have to try it to find out, and don't give up quickly.

What happens when your friends scoff at you and say all kinds of stupid things about you for going to church when you could be out getting high? If you would rather be cool and stoned, get ready for inside time. This is not absolute, but roll the dice enough times and you will crap out.

Again, and I hope to repeat this time and again, it is the friends we make who make the difference between being inside or outside.

Refuse to go along to get along

Can you say "No!" to friends? Or, will you go along with whatever it is, in order to get along?

Can you refuse a friend who wants you to steal something with him? Or beat someone up who owes money, or who looked too long at a girlfriend, or has a new electronic whatever you want, or mug someone who usually has dope on them, and on and on. You know that your friendship may be on the line, or worse, if you refuse. He might even have some way of punishing you, if you don't go along.

What a trap, and things can go this way—no clean way out. A turning point suddenly looms and you are used to caving in, but in a moment something can happen and your world is turned upside down. It happens literally all the time when you go along to get along.

As it has turned out for some—they get beat up and humiliated and thrown out and let go. Being outside is worth it. Ask a few hundred thousand guys, if you could, and you would find out the answer loud and clear.

Read books

If school is not going to happen for you, read books. If you are a graduate, read books. If you can't read, admit it and find a way to learn.

The "self-educated man" is a tag given only with

respect and admiration. And such are the few, the brave, and the smart. You may be too old for high school, but you are not too old to learn to read. Most community colleges have programs for you that are either inexpensive or nearly free.

Reading is working the muscle that fits inside your skull, and reading makes it strong. Women are more impressed with the muscle upstairs than anywhere else.

Maybe start with a daily newspaper or a book sitting on a book shelf at home. Go to a library and start checking out books; be sure to return them on time. Don't let the library check-out process intimidate you—once learned you have it. There is a great big world of knowledge out there, past and present, just waiting to be discovered. Books about everything and anything are awaiting you. A treasured time indeed it is to settle down in a nice chair in a pleasantly appointed reading room, even at the public library, with a best seller in your hands.

Set a goal of going to college

For high school graduates and those with a GED equivalent—What about college?

A college education is a break-out move. This is simply the way it works. No sense fighting it or complaining about it. Not that an education will keep you out of prison, but it is a proven hedge against that possibility.

I attended community colleges for three years and did lots of correspondence courses, and eventually I was able to attend a four year school. My point is that there are inexpensive ways to get a college education.

Find someone to talk to about your anger

There is in each of us a pool of anger that began filling up from about age two. A little at a time, the anger flowed in but rarely out. It inches up the face of the dam and, if not drained away, it will reach the top and overflow.

Anger is that hostile feeling that hits us when we don't get our way. Anger is that rage that comes over us when we have been hurt by someone, maybe a parent, a friend, a relative, a teacher, a minister—someone bigger and more powerful than ourselves. Anger floods in when someone takes something of value from us, and we want revenge.

Revenge—big issue; it is behind so much misery. We seemingly can't let it go, being driven to make things even, or so we think. Life isn't fair, and we will suffer loss—people will betray us, bully us, cheat us, reject us, and hurt us—but it all cycles back when we attempt revenge. Who is the loser in this cycle? The plain answer is the one who takes revenge.

Everybody is angry. I am angry right now just thinking about this subject. I have been bullied, cheated, and robbed, and I have anger down deep. My admitting my anger and talking about it helps me some, and the more I talk about it with someone who understands, the more the anger disappears. Nothing I can do to anybody makes things right. I am helped by the laws of our society. The law says, okay, you will go inside if you steal, rob, mug, kill, etc. and etc., and knowing this helps me put my anger away.

My guess is that anger, aided and abetted by alcohol and dope, has put more people inside than anything else.

Resist the temptation to feel sorry for yourself

You are not the only one in the world who feels like they are screwed from day one. Some may feel they are the worst case ever. That is unlikely, considering the misery there is around the world, but the temptation to feel sorry for yourself would not be unusual.

That temptation must be resisted; it leads to self-medicating and more, and it leads to reckless behavior, not caring what happens to you or anyone else.

When we were kids we thought we would never live to age eighteen, then twenty-one, then twenty-five, considering what we were doing, so what the hell. Or, we convinced ourselves we did not care whether we lived much longer anyway, since we felt so completely awful. These attitudes lead to being inside.

Resist such temptation, because things can change. Mickey Mantle, the great Yankee baseball player, at age 55 said if he had known he would live so long he would have taken better care of himself. Fight to live and turn things around.

Don't give up

Never give up, Refuse to quit. Don't give in, even if you are inside, and if inside, work to get outside.

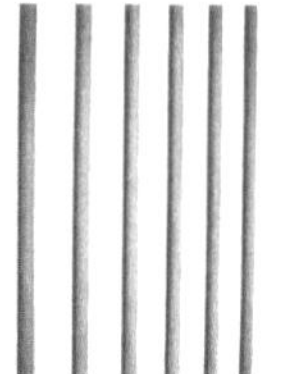

From Harry* – a Former Convict

1. If only I had not failed to realize that my parents concerns about hanging out with the "wrong" crowd, hanging out in the "wrong" places, and doing the "wrong" things weren't based on their desire to make me unhappy, that they were making recommendations to me based on their life experiences, I would not have ended up in prison.

2. Now I know what I would have done, which is talk about my problems with an adult I could trust instead of bottling it all up until it exploded out of me.

3. My experience tells me that life is a struggle, to be sure, but doing the "right" things will result in better outcomes.

4. The #1 thing I would recommend is talk about your feelings, your concerns, your fears, your dreams with an adult you trust.

5. I should have changed my thinking about my future. I believed that the unhappiness I felt as a young man would be a permanent condition. I was wrong.

(*not his real name)

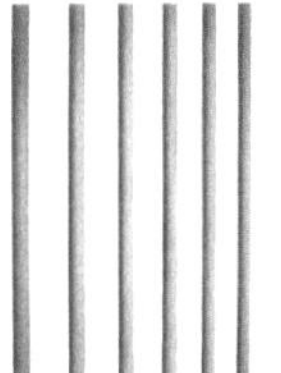

Letter for W. Packer

July 10, 2012

Keith Wattley, Attorney at Law
220 4th Street, Suite 201
Oakland CA 94607

Re. William Packer, H-45835

William Packer asked me to write a letter to the Board
of Prison Terms for him. I understand he is coming up for a
hearing in September or October of this year.

He was instrumental in developing the flag football program at San Quentin State Prison some years back. I was
the volunteer, beige card holder, who sponsored the program. I have been a volunteer at the prison for thirty years,
and sixteen of those years I managed the Baseball team
there.

Proof of Mr. Packer's leadership abilities is seen that
when he left the prison, the program declined. He is a big

presence, and he knows how to organize and stay focused on the essentials. (My son Vernon is currently sponsoring the football program.)

During the third year of the football program, Mr. Packer developed a benign brain tumor, underwent serious surgery, and made a substantial recovery. I observed this process directly and was amazed at his attitude and ability to adjust to very difficult circumstances. Though at one point, being unable to play himself, he nevertheless "showed up" and encouraged the team while walking the sidelines with me.

After Mr. Packer was transferred to another prison, he was frequently mentioned and fondly, in fact, he is still talked about by those who knew him.

Lastly, he has written some helpful material for a book I am writing titled Inside/Outside. My wife Katie and I are the publishers, (earthenvesselmedia.com) and the target of the book is young, at-risk people. Mr. Packer was immediately helpful, and he said he was glad to have a chance to give back.

Sincerely,
Kent Philpott, Sr. Pastor
Miller Avenue Church
Mill Valley, CA 94941

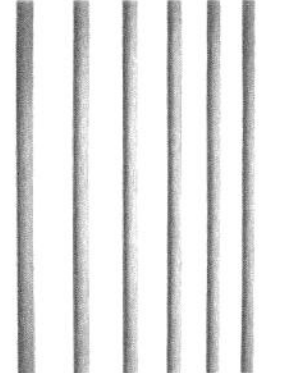

Letter for F. Smith

April 15, 2009

Board Members and Hearing Representatives
Board of Prison Terms and Representatives

Re: Frank Smith,

I am Kent Philpott, pastor of Miller Avenue Baptist Church, Mill Valley, California.

I have been a pastor for nearly forty years. I am a graduate of Golden Gate Baptist Theological Seminary and San Francisco Theological Seminary, as well as Sacramento State University with a degree in psychology.

For twenty-seven years I have been involved in volunteer activities at San Quentin Prison. Since 1997, I have been involved in the sports program and Frank was a part of the team that year and in 1998. In that second year, Frank would umpire at first base and as the first base coach, Frank and I talked together a great deal.

Frank has been very forth coming as to the reasons that got him in trouble and has expressed to me what I consider to be genuine remorse. In addition, Frank has worked hard at changing himself and looking to rehab programs within the prisons he has been at. Over the years I have interacted with a number of convicts who knew Frank, and he is a rare individual who is spoken well of by these people as well as by correctional officers and other prison staff personnel.

Throughout the years, Frank's family has stood with him, and it would be fitting and proper to see him reunited with them. Frank would be an asset to his community. He is skilled in many ways to help others who are at risk. He will be a credit to the state prison system and not an embarrassment.

Sincerely,
Kent Philpott, Sr. Pastor
Miller Avenue Church
Mill Valley, CA 94941

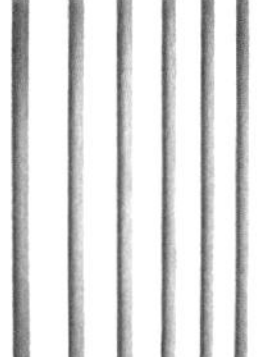

Thinking about the Death Penalty

After reading in the July 2025 edition of The Atlantic an article by Elizabeth Brueig titled "Sin and redemption in America's death chambers," I felt that I had something to contribute:

For 30 years I volunteered at San Quentin Prison, some ten minutes away from where I live in Marin County, nearly 12 of those years doing cell to cell ministry out of the Protestant Chapel, mostly to the North and West Blocks, and then coaching the baseball teams for another 18 years. During that time, I got to know several convicts, some of whom I am still in weekly contact with by means of Gettingout.com. A few of them had been on death row in East Block but were reduced to a level 2, which made it possible for them to come out to play baseball.

Over time, I heard some, not all, of their stories. What I am recalling right now is how many convicts did horrible crimes while messed up on drugs of all sorts, being members (willing or not) of gangs, the names of which I will not mention, and were highly pressured to kill someone, usually of a rival gang. This was often when they were young, even in their late teens.

Murder is murder, the loss of a life, the grief of family and friends—absolutely horrible to have a life brutally ended. Who would disagree?

Must it be "a life for a life?"

Some, as I have heard from or been told about, wanted their lives to end. They hated the idea of spending the rest of their lives in a cell on death row and thought that life ending was better. I am no expert here, but I have had the conversations and read the letters, and so on.

To Elizabeth Brueig, thank you for this article. I am making copies of it to hand out to the congregation.

Kent Philpott, pastor
Miller Avenue Baptist Church
Mill Valley, CA

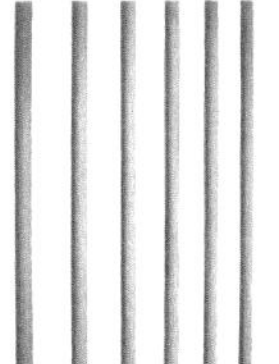

2: Inside Working to Get Outside

Okay, you did not have much of a chance, or no chance, to put into play what was talked about in chapter one. Now I deal with what is happening right now. You are locked up. What a mess! And it may be awhile until you start to develop your mission plan, your reason to go forward and live another day. But you will do so, if only to keep from losing your mind or what is left of it.

Of course, you will bitch and moan for some time. Go ahead. You will want to give it up when you find you are sick and tired of it and have worked yourself into a hole.

Do something. You must do something. First admit that you did the deed that landed you in jail and stop blaming anyone or anything else. All the newly arriving convicts are really innocent, or so the joke goes, but we know better, and that lie has to be rejected. You did it, about 98% of the time, so move on to the next phase—start looking around to see what is available.

At San Quentin there are many programs available. You actually can get rehabilitated, though it sounds like a vapid, made up word as Red said in *Shawshank Redemption*. Rehabilitated is a reality, and this is what the people on parole boards are concerned with. Think about it—no one wants to let you outside until they are convinced or have a sense you are a safe risk. This is totally arbitrary—no one really knows one way or the other, and the politicians are scared to make a mistake. You may think that none of this is necessarily fair, and no one really understands your special circumstances. As best as you are able put that attitude aside, even if it is a little at a time, because it will do you no good to keep it.

To get outside requires work and a lot of it, harder work than most people, inside or outside, have ever done. In the rest of this chapter are some ideas for you. Think about them, maybe for weeks, before you decide they are stupid ideas or unworkable. Maybe there is one idea among them that speaks to you; find that one and then work on getting outside.

Admit you did the deed

This is where it starts. Denial is an early stage of the loss or grieving process. You had a loss, a really big one, and you understandably want to deny it.

For years I went cell to cell in West Block when it was filled with guys wearing orange jump suits, and I can still hear guys yelling in the tiers, "I am not supposed to be here." "This is a mistake." "I never did anything." "You got the wrong guy." And so on. Words and tears and fears for maybe a few days. Then reality begins to set in. No one is listening anyway, no one cares, and no one is going to do anything about anything. The poor cons around you get tired of it and tell you to shut up and threaten to beat the hell out of you or worse.

Some go on for quite a long time telling everyone who will listen to them, and these are few and far between, about how innocent they are or some other sob story. Like taking the beef for your brother or friend or girlfriend or son, or member of the gang, but you, no, you did not do the deed. This goes on longest for those whose crime is sexual in nature—raping or molesting; no one wants to admit these types of crimes. Funny how word leaks out anyway, or more accurately, everybody knows some time before you even get to the lock-up. The worst insult to fellow cons is to try to lie your way out of it.

There is a saying in the Bible, "Let him who is without sin cast the first stone" (John 8:7). With this as the standard, no one, all things being true and equal, would be throwing any rocks at anyone for anything. As Clint Eastwood said in the great western, Unforgiven, to his young partner in crime who is trying to excuse a killing, "Kid, we all got it coming." One of my friends said he was not guilty of the crime which landed him in prison, but he got away with so much else he figured he had it coming anyway. Well, do with that what you want, but it is time to admit the deed.

So now you are doing time, maybe a long time, but you may just live long enough to get out and have some life left. Maybe you figure you will die in the joint, not a pleasant prospect, but you have not given up completely. Some have gone into madness they are in so much despair. Even if you got life without possibility of parole, and inside is all you are going to know, still there is life inside—not the kind of life you want, of course, but life, nevertheless. One thing is sure; there is no moving forward until you admit you did the crime and are now paying the price.

Stop blaming the system

A mindset that is detrimental to cons for decades, is the idea that prisons exist as a business, that people are getting rich off the justice system. This is a familiar theme song, which I have heard countless times and actually bought into myself early on. What it essentially does is focus anger on the whole prison system, perpetuates the anger/hate cycle, and locks you into being a helpless and hopeless victim.

Yes, it seems that laws are heavier and sentences longer for certain kinds of crimes. That is not completely proven; some strides are being made to deal with inequities, but that aside, feeding anger against the "man" is not going to advance the agenda of getting out of prison.

People are indeed making money building prisons, administrating them, and working as correctional officers. One of the strongest unions in California and across the country are the correctional officers' unions. They get what they want, and their demands have been very successful. Prisons and guards would not be needed, if we did not keep breaking the laws of the land, and no civilized society can tolerate the breaking of its developed laws. It is that simple. You break the law, you will pay. And someone has to manage all that, and few really want to get involved. The old cliché nails it: "Someone has to do it," so we pay people, and have to pay them well to do it.

Every new con gets indoctrinated with the blame-the-system mantra. Many grab hold of it and run with it, and the result is moving in the direction of institutionalization, a frame of mind that does not build one up or help move one along the path of getting outside.

Dealing with time

You knew what it was like to be outside with freedom, family, friends, and the good times; now these are gone. You did what you wanted when you wanted, even when no one was making you do anything. Now you know what some think is cruel and unusual punishment.

Time inside can feel like forever. Thirty years, maybe even fifty with the three strikes thing in California, but whatever the number, it can torment you each damned minute. Two years can seem unbearable. It is different for different people.

Some are used to doing time, starting when a teenager, and others have no record and no trouble, but one day it happened, and life will never be the same. Time and more time; little or no light at the end of the tunnel.

Time is best done one day at a time. You have a day in front of you, and it may consist of no more than being in your cell. Set a goal like reading a chapter in a book, or attempting to have a conversation with a cellie, even an officer, but a few words exchanged with someone. Maybe write a page in a journal, even if you know you won't be able to take it with you when you are moved to another part of the institution or to a new lock-up all together. It is the effort that counts, that immediate effort and not an end result.

A guy who played on one of the Giants teams in 2008 said he got by day by day by not having any expectations. If anything happened out of the boring ordinary, then he was surprised and gratified, even if just a little. You can't count on prison life to go smoothly, considering fights, new wardens showing up, and other unpleasant little things like a flooding of the tiers, or a race riot, and a dozen other weird things, many of which have taken place in the chow hall or on the yard. No expectations means fewer disappointments, and a greater ability to take delight in really small things.

Ever hear about the religious monks who spent their lives in the Egyptian deserts during the fourth century and beyond—akin to a self-imposed prison? Or maybe think of the political prisoners who were guilty of no crime except having a different opinion than the people in power. Or those who had everything stripped away from them by a natural disaster. Or a paralyzed war veteran unable to move a finger or toe. They learned the secret of solitude; they moved from loneliness to being able to be okay with being alone. There is great strength here. Some of the finest and most mature people I have ever known have been able to be content living out their time in harsh conditions. Heroes who did not go mad, treated others with respect, knew who they were, and achieved something with their lives, even though nobody else would ever know it.

Dealing with your anger

Anger—this is usually the biggest challenge. It is the phase of the loss process that lasts the longest, maybe even for years. Being filled with anger is not going to serve you well. It is more likely to keep you miserable and make your time worse.

At first, anger can help deal with the enormity of the loss. At the same time it prevents you from feeling the pain that is deep inside. Anger can also go way down. If left to fester, it can cause severe depression, strong thoughts of suicide, and uncontrollable rage toward everyone around you. Anger has got to be dealt with, or it will keep you from getting back outside.

There is much to be angry about. Maybe there is anger toward parents, or friends who let us down, maybe turned us over, or left us holding the proverbial bag. Then there are the cops, the attorneys, the judges, the juries, the whole screwed justice system—yes there is truth to it—but focusing on that will get you no good thing except more grief.

No doubt there were some major betrayals, bad enough

to possibly cause you to commit mayhem and murder. No matter how justified that would seem, still this anger must be dealt with and subdued.

How about self-loathing, which is anger directed toward yourself? "What a dumb bastard I am. How could I be so stupid? I must be the worst that ever was. I ought to kill myself I am so worthless. I only deserve death and hell. I am unlovable. I am no good, a real child of the devil." That may sound extreme, but self-anger may be more difficult to deal with than any other kind.

We can grow up being angry, but often the anger is rarely dealt with. We pile it all up in a heap. A way to look at it is to imagine a pool, like a swimming pool, and we start early on in our lives filling up the pool with anger. It happens because we don't know what to do with it all. We don't learn how to apologize, hardly anyone apologizes to us, bitterness and resentments grow and accumulate, the slights and downright dirty and awful things people have done to us—they get tossed into the pool.

Many people who end up in prison have been abused by a parent or other relative. Truly awful and criminal acts happened; they went unpunished, unmentioned, undealt with—it all just accumulates and goes putrid into the pool. One day it spills over.

How is the pool emptied? No magic can do it or cheap three-easy-step formulas will work. What works is talking it out—talking out the hurt, telling the stories of the wrongs, over and over, looking at them from one angle and then another, talking out the anger with someone who will listen and not counsel or advise.

A whole therapeutic industry has risen up around our need to talk things out. It is legitimate and necessary. There are not many therapists in most joints, but there may be some. Check them out. Or perhaps a friend discovered in prison might be reliable enough and safe enough to talk to. Yet again, it might work to have someone to write to on the outside who will read the words of your nightmare. Prayer is good—you are not wasting time talking to God. Or start putting the anger out in a journal. The point is that you can find a way to empty the pool, and it will make all the difference. It frees you up to begin looking for other means that will lead to finding yourself on the outside again.

Programs

As I mentioned before, San Quentin has a lot of programs, a real smorgasbord. This is a rare exception, however, and there is not much going on at level three and four prisons. With inmate numbers down to level two, some prisons make programs available.

Early in their incarceration, most inmates have high numbers, a two or a three, and all they have is their cell, maybe a little caged yard, and an occasional visit. Pretty bare, and this is the time that is the hardest. The boredom is almost crushing. Now is the time to be working on yourself, making admissions to yourself about the crime, and your whole life really, starting to flush anger out of the pool, and developing some hope. In time, the numbers will go down, and good things can begin to open up.

Take advantage of anything and everything. Take classes you would normally hate and totally disregard what anyone else says. New material to learn can be frustrating, and there is no growth without a level of frustration—that is just how it is. You can fail a course or a class and it does not make you a failure.

Drug and alcohol programs—go for them. Whatever you can fit in, do it. I wish every prison had the wide variety of programs that prisons like San Quentin have, but they don't, so you might have to build your own program.

The list of possibilities for programs might include ones that deal with drug and alcohol addiction, domestic violence, racial issues, how to make it on the outside, families on the outside, anger management, and so on. Most prison libraries will have some books on these issues, or they can be obtained. I have known guys who started their own groups of like-minded people and met informally on the yard.

Deal with your racism

Divisions, factions, races, gangs, tribes, we-they—hopelessly dividing people one from another. Though all human beings are connected in many ways, conflicts are a constant and reconciliations infrequent.

Are you a racist? Probably you are, if not up front, then on your arm, or the chest, or the back; maybe writ large across your forehead. You have a "we" that you are fiercely attached to. As far as you are concerned, it is your family, your safety, your access to extra goodies, the way you do business and survive. All understood. You may keep it quiet so as not to be validated, but you have an identity in the block, in the chow hall, and on the yard.

You may not be able to escape it, or opt out, or quit, but you can still deal with your racism, an attitude that may have caused you to get where you are now. It will certainly impede your getting out and will definitely not be an asset once you do get out.

My "research" tells me that most guys would have nothing to do with a gang based on race, or any other reason, if they could avoid it. Trapped is trapped, but you must come to terms with reality. What means the most to you, the group or your freedom? Sometimes you can't have both.

Behind racism is hatred and anger, which can be so

deeply rooted that it would take a crow bar or dynamite to dislodge them. Some joints have programs on this topic attended by cons who know that the racism within is eating them up. Being hated and hating are not the way to live.

At San Quentin there are team sports that are interracial, or at least they are supposed to be. Playing a sport with guys from another race reveals they are just like us—surprise, surprise. It is incredible to see what can happen. I wish all prisons could do this, but likely only Level one or two prisons could do it.

So, you get out, then it is back to the gang, and part of doing business is battling the competitors, much of which is fueled by racism. Of course, even within races there is racism, maybe depending on where you come from or where you moved to or which gang you decided to join, and it ushers you into illegal activity, to put it mildly.

Hate and anger are the killers behind the killers. They have got to go. Consider a basic tenet linked to most if not all religious and spiritual groups, "Do unto others as you would have them do to you." Applying that principle could change your life. An effort to live with such a principle can help get you outside and stay outside.

Understanding COs

Guards, bulls, turn-keys, correctional officers—these are the people cons have to interact with. They can be male, female, gay, straight, mean, nice, and completely awful. It is incredible to have a gay guard, or a gay or straight female officer stand and watch the guys shower, and sometimes while making nasty comments. Of course, the officers will take some abuse for it, maybe a distasteful display, but bottom line—no one gets blessed much.

Over the years I have seen normal everyday people come into the prison, put on the uniform and badge, and for a while act okay, but then you see them turn into something else. How does this happen?

Prison is a stressful place for con and freeperson alike. The whole idea of prison is discomforting. Prison is a dangerous place, and you never know when violence will break out.

Con and guard alike will be stressed out, maybe much of the time, and not even realize it. Being under prolonged tension will change anybody. And truth be told, convicts can treat officers terribly, set them up for all kinds of mischief, and generally make their lives miserable. Should it be expected that harassed, even brutalized people, can remain cool, calm, and collected?

Cons expect way too much of the prison staff. Yes, most are there for the money and the benefits, but such is not a reason to despise them and treat them with contempt. And after all, ours is the kind of country where people are to be free to seek their own advantage in a lawful manner. In the military, those of us who served were taught to respect the rank regardless of who was wearing it. Cons will be far better served to copy a GI's way of doing things, if for no other reason than that the officer has a chance to be a real human being. And remember: respect begets respect.

Little by little

A word needs to be said now considering the huge mountain just thrown out in front of you—take it a little bit at a time.

Books are written, films made, and plays staged about the life of a person who can overcome strong inner thoughts and emotions such as hatred, anger, and racism. Probably few will do it, but it can be approached and that over a lifetime. However, you have to start now, even if it is under cover.

If possible, start talking to someone not in your group. Little by little. You might find that you are not alone in wanting to get past the prejudice that has plagued you all your life. Give it a try, take the risk; it is worth the effort and maybe a beating. Think of the programs you will not be able to engage in if you have to avoid direct contact with enemies. It will be you and your bunch living a life of fear and revenge. Not much of a life, and one that will surely keep you inside.

How to blow the whistle

It is not uncommon to be compromised by a correctional officer or other state employee. I know at least two cons at San Quentin who got written up, because they refused marriage proposals—of course, the charge was that the guys came onto the women. Then there was the officer who routinely molested young new guys just coming into the system. One player on a team I managed in the late 1990s got so tired of having to hide from the officer that he finally told another officer what was going on and in a short time he, the con, was transferred to another prison, one far away from civilization.

It is a dicey situation to be sure, but there are times when you have to stand your ground. Usually when you let a little stuff slide, it only gets worse.

Sending out a kite is one way to do things, at least get the problem before an investigative unit. You can expect that people will start butt-covering, but the mischief may just end up in the hands of someone who really cares and is not afraid to act. But making what might seem like threats to a trouble maker, with witnesses around, is not sound policy. Everything must be done decently and in order. Of course, if your own hands are dirty, the whole thing might end up being detrimental to you—a write-up going into your jacket.

Probably the best way to go is to confide in a counselor, though this might take a while, especially if you are a new arrival. I have found that teachers in the education/recreation department are trustworthy people, too.

Over my thirty years as a volunteer at San Quentin I have met many correctional officers who can be counted on. Cons often make the mistake of the we/they mentality, automatically assuming the cops are against you. By talking to an old timer at the prison you can usually find out who is reliable.

Make time count for you

Time can be on your side. Perhaps never before have you been in a situation to spend so much time thinking and reflecting upon your life. Some literally grow up in prison. They work past the wild teen age years when the brain chemistry pushed them to ridiculous risk taking. There were periods when it did not cross the mind what might be the result of living recklessly and all the while being drunk, stoned, and crazy.

Start growing up, but you will not, if you are doing dope inside. Time will work against you, if you give up working on improvement to get high. At some point you must face the reality that is now yours—you are in prison with Bubba and the boys and for a long time. You want to escape in your mind, but look around you at the cons who went that way—they are sick, crazy, and getting worse every day.

You can be a man worthy of respect in prison. Some of the most mature and upstanding people I have ever known are lifers, cons who set out on the road less travelled. Stand back then and do what you want to do, and if it is going along to get along, then it might be another ten or twenty years before you realize that you must make time work for you.

Keeping your mind in the game

Living is like being an athlete; you have to keep focused. Being locked up for a long period of time makes it is easy to get distracted, diverted into things that do not build you up nor increase your chances to get outside.

Those who have played sports learn to keep their head in the game. You have a game to play, and that is to get out of prison. Focus on it, give it 110%, don't dog it or get lazy—you are always moving forward.

In baseball we say, "See the ball, hit the ball. See the ball, catch the ball." Simple little formula, but the guy who can do it will be successful or at least do better than they would otherwise. Thus it is in prison—keep your eye on the goal, which is walking through the gate and away from everything that is now behind you.

Sex in prison

You knew I was going to get around to this at some point. This is a sticky one, since there are several different points of view. That said, there are still a few things to mention that may be of help to someone.

Hormones are powerful and totally addictive. Going to jail young you are going to have to face the sex issue; but everyone has to deal with the reality that the body keeps on making the feel-good juices for most if not all our lives.

A prison has its ranks, and the child molesters are at the bottom, a little up from the rapists, and the homosexuals are in this mix. I am not assigning any moral judgments here, but I thought it is necessary to at least bring the subject up.

It is understood that the sexual drive can drive you nuts. Watching television and internet sites and reading the newspapers and magazines and seeing all the flesh and the loving couples playing in bed—How much can you take?

Some say to do your sex by yourself. Some say avoid it all together if you can, and if you fail, don't become discouraged and depressed. Then there is the "sublimate" crowd who suggests channeling your chemical/mind drives into things like sports, music, drama, reading, art, and so on. What is the best way to go? Frankly, you will have to figure it out for yourself, and it might be different at different stages in your life.

Dealing with set backs

Not everything will go well—a fact of life. I have discovered that I am more often shocked when things turn out well. There will also be setbacks, like in the old saying, "One step forward, two steps back."

Just when you get settled into some positive directions, along comes a 115, maybe the hole, or even a transfer. You feel like giving up. Or, maybe a change of a job that makes being part of that new program impossible. How about a new warden showing up and cutting back on programs to show how tough he or she is. There are real reasons why some cons get broken down and become institutionalized—they give up, and I do not disparage them, because I know how easy it would be to go that way.

Setbacks are bound to come your way. Count on it, but keep moving forward. You may be discouraged for some time, which would only be natural. Maturity may be measured by how big a hit you can take and still get up and go at it again.

Avoid magical thinking—an easy or quick out

There is no magical way to get outside the walls, which are thick and high, not to mention the fact that they are dotted with gun towers. It is unlikely that the political climate will change to such an extent you will be driven down to the main gate in a limo. It is going to be a slog, a hard road ahead, and no "get out of jail free" card is going to come in the mail or handed to you through the bars.

Keeping hope alive is an internal process, a refusing to give in to what present circumstances are indicating. Expect a fight, disappointments, setbacks, and understand your best efforts may not result in any reward. The fight may be the whole thing, the sole benefit, which must be enough. Anything more is a gift.

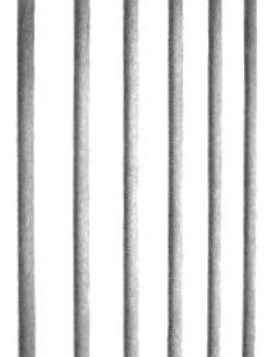

On Overdose Deaths*

Formerly incarcerated Americans face a significantly higher risk of fatal drug overdose compared to the general population, with studies indicating this risk is 10 to 40 times higher in the immediate, 2-week period following release. Drug overdose is the leading cause of death for this population upon re-entry into the community.

Why Post-Release Overdose Risk is Extremely High

• Reduced Tolerance: While incarcerated, individuals often stop using substances, leading to a drastic decrease in tolerance. If they use the same amount of drugs upon release as they did previously, their bodies cannot handle it, leading to a high likelihood of fatal overdose.

• The "First Two Weeks" Danger: The risk of fatal overdose is highest within the first 48 hours to two weeks of release.

• Lack of Addiction Treatment (MOUD): Many correctional facilities do not provide medications for opioid use disorder (MOUD)—such as methadone or buprenorphine—which can reduce the risk of death by 75%.

•   Re-entry Stress and Environment: Returning to communities with limited housing, unemployment, and high access to drugs creates intense, immediate pressure that triggers relapse.

•   Limited Access to Naloxone: Many individuals are not provided with naloxone (a drug that reverses opioid overdoses) upon release, and they may be in environments where peers are not trained to assist them.

Key Findings on Overdose Risk

•   40x Higher Risk: A North Carolina study found that former inmates were 40 times more likely to die of an opioid overdose within the first two weeks post-release.

•   Heroin-Specific Risk: For heroin specifically, the risk of overdose death for formerly incarcerated individuals increased to 74 times the norm in the first two weeks.

•   Leading Cause of Death: Overdose is not just a high risk, but the leading cause of death among people recently released from prison.

•   Persistent Risk: Even one year after release, overdose death rates remain 10-18 times higher than the general population.

Interventions to Save Lives

Research shows that continuing, or initiating, medications for opioid use disorder (MOUD) during, and immediately after, incarceration is the most effective way to cut the risk of death by up to 75%. Effective reentry programs that include immediate access to treatment and social support are crucial in reducing these preventable deaths.

Contributing factors include, "Poor housing, unemployment, psychosocial problems, and barriers to health care," that cause this deadly reality. These Americans deserve better. They need to know that they are not forgotten and that they have paid their debt to society. The only way the United States can truly improve on the effects of the opiate epidemic is together. As a team.

*Found mostly at the Justice Community Overdose Innovation Network (JCOIN: jcointc.org) and Vera: Overdose Deaths and Jail Incarceration (vera.org)

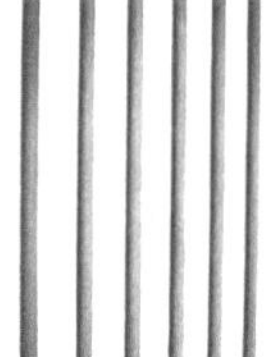

Christmas at the Q

Having spent 10 holiday seasons inside the 25-foot walls of San Quentin State Prison, I can assure you that one of the many things that makes life inside a maximum-security penitentiary different and difficult is that the holidays creep up on you so very quickly. For most of the men incarcerated behind the walls--whether they are regular prisoners doing various stretches, lifers, or on death row--the holiday season is emotionally very rough. In December, more than other times of the year, it's not uncommon for people to rub each other's nerves the wrong way. But good things can happen, too.

One particular year, for example, a fellow inmate played Santa Claus for the kids that came into the prison during visiting hours. The men who undertook the Toys for Tots campaign during the holiday season had spent a number of prideful moments putting this program together. This program allowed the men to give the underprivileged visiting kids an opportunity to receive toys, gifts, cards, and candies, among other treats. If not for the Toys for Tots campaign, these children would not have received any type of gifts during that holiday season.

As for the fellow prisoner who was chosen to be Santa Claus that year, he had spent a number of days putting the costume together, making sure that the white beard was smoothed out, and ready for the big day. On the day Christmas came, this proud Santa was out in the visiting room with all of these happy little kids. Imagine the smiles on their faces. What makes this particular scene unique is that even in a maximum-security prison, the men behind the walls were able to give back and bring joy to a little one. It is a remarkable thing to watch.

Besides Santa, each year many inmates also dress up as elves. This makes Christmas time at San Quentin an especially festive occasion. The inmates who usually walk tough on the yard now wear elf uniforms with tights and red ornaments around their necks. The kids respond to the banter and have such fun playing with the elves. And then there's Santa, who's got candy canes, ornaments, and lots of other stuff to give out. He has gifts that are wrapped, and gifts that are unwrapped. He hands out toys to the excited kids, who climb over each other to get them. Now, I'm not an advocate who says that we should do away with prisons; in fact, some of the most dangerous people in the state of California are locked-up behind the walls of San Quentin. But that shouldn't denigrate the feelings that people have during the holiday season. For one day at least, Santa, his helpers and everyone else aren't simply inmates--they're human beings.

Christmas Eve was also a time when some of the inmates bonded around what was on television. The local PBS station would show nothing but a fireplace with a Yuletide log, accompanied by Christmas songs sung by Bing Crosby, Burl Ives or Frank Sinatra. This being the big event of the evening, all the prisoners would lay in their bunks waiting for the log to make its first crackle, at which point the cellblock would erupt with shouting and whooping and hollering. Some of the men even had a pool on the exact time when the first pop would occur. Many of the men bless the Yule log on TV during Christmastime.

San Quentin is more than 150 years old, and many a Christmas has passed through its dank and dusty walls. It's always on the verge of being condemned, but over 6,000 prisoners will be spending the holidays there this year. As for me, for the first time in 25 years, I'm out in the community, where I'll be in the embrace of my loved ones, family, and friends. Even though I expect the coming holidays to be much brighter and more cheerful than any I've experienced in a long time, I'll still be thinking of this year's Santa, his elves, and the Yuletide log in the fireplace.

By J.T. Gottlieb

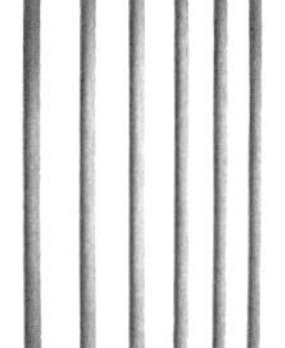

3: Staying Outside

The greater challenge begins now. You are an ex-con, probably on parole and that for as many as 5 years. Make your parole agent happy; do what he or she says, regardless whether you think it is fair or not.

No matter what, do the required program. Expect the first few days to be the most difficult. It will take a whole lot of self-control to fight the urge to get loaded and get back with the "homies." Your first priority is to use the $200 of gate money right; if you don't have a place to stay, find a low-rent hotel. Then, make sure you have groceries. For the last however many years, the state has provided you food and shelter, now you're on your own. So be smart and frugal.

You certainly are a tough guy, but how do you avoid landing back in the joint? Guys want to do crime with you. They want to be like you. You have all the markings of a veteran con with maybe your arms "sleeved down" with tattoos. Sure, this makes you intimidating to some normal "squares" who may call the police even if you haven't done anything. Try to tone down your look with long sleeve shirts, and if you have tattoos on your neck and face, think seriously about removal. Some places do removal for free. Another thought is cover-up make up, but the important thing here is for you to blend in with the outside society. At least this way, you can be both "tough" and smart.

If your program is—get sex and dope, make up for lost time, get money the easy way—you will be back inside soon. Think about it—the civilized world we live in will not tolerate you; you will have to be taken off the streets. You know for a fact you would not want to live in such a world much less try to raise a family in a crime infested neighborhood patrolled by bangers and thugs.

To hell with being cool. Being an ex-con is not something to be proud of. Dress like you are ready to go to work, anywhere. Hanging with the homies will be a cheap ticket for a bus ride back to that tiny cell. You must, and I mean MUST find others to be friends with. It does no good to all sink together. One saved person can perhaps help others out of the goo.

It is time to grow up, to be a man or a woman. It is time to be an actual adult instead of a kid. Yes, the experts say that you are at the age, mentally and emotionally, as when you first started getting loaded. Maybe so, but it is now time to grow up, therefore, sober and clean is the only way to go. Avoid putting yourself at risk of going back.

You want to be a hero. Go to school, get a job; walk away from drugs and alcohol. Say NO to drugs and alcohol. We all know dope and booze are behind 80% of the reasons people go to jail. Either you do something stupid while stoned or you do something stupid to get stoned.

You have never been in a bigger fight in your life. It compares to a race riot on a level IV prison yard. You may not want to be involved but you can't help it. The fight seems to come from every side. And getting knocked down means getting back up, and as often as it happens. You may feel like shit sometimes, but get back up and fight.

Have you been institutionalized?

Being inside a long time can institutionalize you, meaning that you have learned to be comfortable in a place where the rules have been set and life has a predictable routine. It is like being in the military—you learn the ropes, you learn to cope, you learn to survive, you learn to thrive—steady, controlled, safe to a degree, and outside of that regimentation, life can be hard or even overwhelming.

It's not your fault if you fell into the routine. Remember how upset you got when a new sergeant came along and changed the rules, or when a correctional officer did things one way then changed and did them another? It can throw your game off. Now outside you must develop your own routine. It is smart to look into a transitional housing situation, which can serve as an initial safety net. The time spent there will be well worth it.

Be as patient and flexible as you can be. If you are afraid, talk to someone about it. Who cares what others think of you; you are focused on staying out and everything must be sacrificed. You are armed with information now, about the whole institutional thing, and you can look for the indicators yourself. Being like a normal person who walks around and talks to people and does stuff may seem more than you can do without something to help balance out the blizzard of emotions you are fighting. But experience shows that you can make it, not easily, but you can make it. Just knowing what to expect goes a long way.

Friends are huge now

We are heavily influenced by our friends; it goes without saying. If your friends smoke dope, and so on, you likely will too—it only makes sense. If they gang bang, you probably will. If they hang out at the clubs and party, you are going to go along. If you ride around checking the hot spots late weekend nights looking for action, do you suspect you might find more than you wanted? If they have a criminal mentality when it comes to getting money, would you be able to resist? If those you hand with treat boyfriends or girlfriends in abusive ways, might you also copy that behavior?

The answers to these questions are not always obvious and you are lying to yourself if you are thinking you would be different, that you alone would have the ability to avoid the dangers. When you hang with the wrong crowd, you welcome danger and the likelihood of your going back to prison increases.

Old friends are comfortable and right there. You get with the old bunch and tell yourself you deserve a good time since you have been locked up so long. Self-pity is dangerous. You missed what you missed; but you can miss more.

And a caution here: if you have been in jail more than five years and have not used during that time, the chemicals in the brain that drive us toward wanting more of the same have pretty much disappeared. But less than five years, drugs like meth will still be messing with our minds acting as a lure back to getting wired again even though you don't understand it. And off you go. This is good science so take heed.

Be aware that there will be a terrific yearning to get drunk, stoned, and stupid almost immediately after hitting the streets again. If this is not resisted, and if dope played a role in the crimes(s), then your parole agent might just spring a surprise testing on you. But what often happens that once the weird chemicals reach the brain, about two seconds later, the craving for more sets in and by the time you have run out of money, dope, and energy, you are on your way back in and maybe with a new beef rather than a violation.

Maybe it depends on how badly you want to stay out. Jail house wisdom has it that people don't wake up to the fact they have wasted their lives until about age 35, some say 45. Whatever it might be, the issue comes down to maturity and strength of character. Some simply cannot say no to their friends; pleasing them means more than staying outside. Odd, strange, baffling—right, but it is true nevertheless.

Some of the people you might call friends will actually want to bring you down; some may want you off the streets again, for all kinds of personal reasons. Who can you really trust? Ask a con who has been around for a long time and you might find the answer to be—Darn few if any. And local cops may want to see you back inside, too. You may be a target now so be smart about your movements and who you are friends.

Getting new friends is not easy however, but it can be done. What it takes is the courage to go to new and safer places, be with safer people, and risk new challenges. It can be special too, a real adventure. It might take some investigative work on your part, but it could prove to be worth it.

Stay away from the corner hangouts at night

Constantly in the newspapers are stories about somebody getting gunned down, either intentionally or accidentally, while going out to the local store for supplies who then end up being in the wrong place at the wrong time. Those places are like magnets for people who are unhappily at the bottom of the barrel and as much as you might think this is prejudicial thinking, it is wise to acknowledge what you know to be true. Weird attracts weird; if a person acts weird they probably are weird, and more importantly, dangerous.

Resist self-pity

Right about now you may be tempted to self-pity. You might complain you are trapped. You might think, "Hell, what am I supposed to do, stay home and watch television all day long? Give up all my friends? Have nowhere to go?"

This may all be true for some time; at least it is better than going back to prison. There is an adjustment period. Now you have to sit down and think. Yes, you did not have a good start in life; yes, you wasted some years, some good young years; yes, others have families and jobs, homes even, and here you are with nothing and no good thing coming. This may all be true, but you are outside and that is what it is all about.

You may be living in transitional housing, the old halfway house, and if so, that is a good thing. Without such ex-cons often do not make it for a day. The money they got when released went mostly for dope by the time they got off the bus. No joke and it is not funny. Talk about a waste.

Take patiently what you have in front of you whether provided by the state, the feds, or a community agency. It is intended to prevent you from going back inside. Think about it: it costs lots of money for you to go through the justice system and then be incarcerated. And prison is not a growth industry by choice, only by necessity. People don't usually go to prison because the man is running a con-game; people go to prison because they broke the law and have become a menace to others. You will be smart to ditch the old conspiracy theories.

Many become cynical about all the people involved

in the criminal justice system. Fact is that everyone that somehow touches it becomes brutalized, not just the convict. From top down, from judge to a guard on the yard, it is a dirty business, and it changes everybody, and mostly for the worst. However, there are lots of people in the system and lots of people who run rehab and transitional places who have your best interest in mind. Yes, as wild as it might seem, there are people who care. Give them a chance and be patient with them. Listen to them and be humble. That old hard core attitude is an enemy of yours and it is best to put it away.

Dress so as not to scare the hell out of normal folk

Now you have gone to meddling with my life—I am gonna dress how I want to dress. Right, you can do that, and you might as well paint a target on your back too.

Hoodies, gang banger attire—typical, youngster stuff, but not for men—it is no longer cool. Talk about being a target!

Have you known people who want to intimidate an ex-con to show how tough they are? Do you think that a prospective employer might be reluctant to hire an ex-con, especially one who looks like one? Do you suppose that "normal" people might be afraid of hanging out with guys who almost seem to have a sign on them that says, "Don't tread on me."

Kids want to look tough and cool, men don't need to. The self assured person does not have to have clothes to prove anything. It takes some giving up of what might be described as undermining views of ourselves in favor of a life style you might once have looked down upon, but it is still true, outside is better than inside.

Prison—a career move?

A career move? Yes indeed, for some it is. Prison at least

means a dry place to sleep, three meals a day, medical and dental care (however lousy), and people to be with. But this is also dangerous thinking; it is a kind of giving up.

Prison is an option for those who are not going to make it on the outside for any number of reasons. It is a sad state of affairs but true. This book is for those who want to stay on the outside and to do so they will want to find a career, a job to do, one that will pay the rent and buy the food.

Getting a job is not easily done, obviously, and this is understood. It may take everything you have to pull a career out of an empty hat. There is school; night adult classes are just about everywhere and very affordable. If you don't read or write so well—this tells you what classes to sign up for. Pride has got to go; it is a barrier to getting done what needs to be done. Let people scoff, and those who do are not your real friends. There are union halls; often they have apprenticeship programs and are looking for people who are willing to work. Check out the newspapers, Craig's List, and bulletin boards at supermarkets and laundries. And, there are people out there who may even come alongside and help you figure out what to do. Do not be silent and do not be afraid to ask for help.

If you have been down a long time the modern techy culture may be scary to you. You are not alone. The world has drastically changed and electronics, especially computers, have transformed the world and it is good and right to jump into it. Cell phones—you are probably up to speed there already.

A computer itself is cheaper than you might think and there are classes to learn how to make it work for you. You may consider it a necessary evil, but if you can find it within yourself at all, give computers a shot.

Be willing to work your way up

There was a comedian whose most famous line was, "I get no respect." He was such a dimwit that everyone knew why he didn't—he hadn't earned any.

Respect is owed is some cases. I must respect the humanity, the office, the position, the authority, regardless of who is behind the badge or name plate. Respect to whom respect is due is an old saying, but personal respect is not automatic—it must be earned.

A new hire always get the crap hours and dirtiest jobs; this is how it goes in the real world. An honest and hard worker earns respect and starts getting better hours, is by-passed on the scummy jobs, and starts making more money. It takes time of course to adjust and settle in. Be patient with the boss, other workers, and yourself.

In almost every job there are ways of cheating, taking advantage, and cutting corners. These get found out eventually, and then jobs end. A good man is hard to find and when one is, good things happen.

What is the goal here, what is the objective? It is not necessarily to get wealthy; few people ever do so, this 1% of the population. Most of us are 99%ers and okay with that. What you want is to have a meaningful life, pay your bills, and have a place to live and food to eat. There might even be some extra goodies, but the goal is to live an honest life and be respected by our family, our friends, and those who know us at all. It is all earned; it is not owed.

Live simply and don't compare yourself with others

Growing up poor is not so bad and the majority do, some poorer than others of course. Only nuts think that whoever dies with the most toys wins. That is purely crazy thinking and defeating in the long run. A simple life, honest and open before the world, a clean conscience, with nothing to fear when someone comes knocking on the door—this is true wealth.

Others will have more than you do, maybe the bulk of the population will have more material things than you do. So what? Think of it: The more you have, the more you have to protect. The more you have, the more you have to worry about. The more you have, the more people there will be who will want to take it away from you, one way or another. What you want is freedom and to be outside. There is no comparison.

Avoid debt

Debt is a killer; it can weigh you down with a worry that tortures the soul. From some considerable experience, hear a bit of what may be wisdom.

Avoid debt, if at all possible. Sometimes it is not, like for a big purchase, a necessary item, be sure however that you can handle the payments. Oh, by the way, avoid and like the plague, casinos, race tracks, and any and all forms of gambling including taking the odds on sporting events. In prison you probably have seen the misery of those whose gambling debts got them in real trouble. One way of staying away from the growing monthly payments—if you can't buy it with cash, don't buy it. Cash only is wise policy.

Credit cards—do you have to have them? You may think so, but think again. It becomes to many another source of easy money. That kind of debt with crush you. Yes, I carry two cards, a gas card and then a regular card just in case, but I keep the balance low and do my best to pay off the cards totally every month. A lot of regular type folk have resorted to various forms of so-called while collar crime to get themselves out of a self made mess.

Get a bank account and avoid the check cashing joints, a slime ball deal, and utterly reject the corner loan businesses, which are more of the same.

Reject quick and "easy" ways to make a buck. A friend drops by and has a sure deal, you only have to drive, or pick something up, or make a call…you know how it works and pretty quick you are in. The whole thing it may not even be illegal, not totally on the up and up, but even still, as we all know, there is no free lunch. We are to be as wise as a serpent and harmless as a dove. (Someone really famous said that.)

Be honest about your past

Refuse to be looking over your shoulder. We are who we are and we have been who we have been. No changing the past; it is the future we focus on now.

People you will meet, employers, teachers, neighbors, prospective spouses—maybe they all don't have to know your past, but in the computer age with the huge amount of information available on the net, it is virtually impossible to keep everything from view. Better to be upfront than have to explain later. Besides being straight at first means you don't have to tell a series of lies trying to fill in the blanks for the last however many years.

It is not necessary to disclose the crime, but it can get sticky. If you can, without scaring others to death or causing them to start holding you at arm's length—be as forthcoming as you feel safe in doing. We are not obligated to answer every question or fill in all the details. It is quite boring anyway, but you really want to live without fear of having your past live catch up with you like the politicians have to.

Be careful though with youngsters who are impressionable and might see you as a hero of sorts. In many places, if you say you have been in prison, especially if it happens to have been a well known joint, you know how kids will think you are a big deal, especially the girls. Put that sort of false glamour away as you might be encouraging someone toward a life of misery, or death. You can tell your story all right and with a lesson included, not a scold or a lecture, but laying it in between the lines about the wasted years inside.

Hold your head up

Most people are very sensitive about what others think of them. You think—well, they know I am an ex-con and inside they think I am a bad person despite the smile on their face. Truth is, you cannot help what others think about you, but you can refuse to be brought low by what others may have in their heads.

This is not a call to arrogance, and you do not want to despise others on the basis of your own fears. People think what they will, but refuse to be cowed or intimidated. Hold your head up as a person of character. You are out and intend to stay out.

Again, it will take time to demonstrate who you are since respect is earned not owed. Little by little the process moves forward.

What about a slip?

Few are able to clean up right away and completely, after all we are not dealing with fantasy land here. If there are problems, instead of covering up, go for help. If you have developed a bit of a relationship with a parole officer, you may find that to be of value and may discover help and not a ticket back in.

Ministers can be a real source of help. They have a duty

to hold confidence and most of the time they will honor that and provide some substantial encouragement.

There are other health care professionals that may be available also. Do not hide, deceive, and play other games—it will only be a matter of time then. Be proactive right away and seek help. Pride is the enemy when things go awry and pride will be the gate opener back inside.

Others will see your example and be encouraged

You hear the phrase, "giving back to the community." Many convicts do just this. We are acquainted with IMPACT, which means, Incarcerated Men Putting Away Childish Things, started by a former chaplain of San Quentin, Earl Smith. When members get out they often are able to find a support group and be able to be part of a community of people who receive and give support and encouragement. These guys are giving back and you can too.

Kids often have few if any adults to look up to, adults who have their best interests at heart. You can be such a one, especially when you have shown yourself, as well as others, that you can live a good and upright life. We have fewer and fewer heroes to look up to; you may be one of those others look up to.

The end of the story has not been written

Every moment is merely a snapshot in time. We may know what lies behind that photo, the life that was lived, but we know nothing of what may lie ahead.

We all have a story, some not so pretty, but we may build a new story line, one we can be pleased to see released to the public. We have not reached the end of the story, the credits may be a long way off yet, and there is time to reinvent or interrupt the previous plot in the story.

The best story is the one that ends with a twist, a dramatic, or maybe not so dramatic, crisis that makes the audience experience resolution. They then go out feeling good inside and ready to tell their friends to go see the film. This is your challenge: to reinvent yourself and have a dramatic twist to your life.

Your story is not completed yet, more will be written. And it is the end of the story that is most memorable. You may have an academy award winner in you yet.

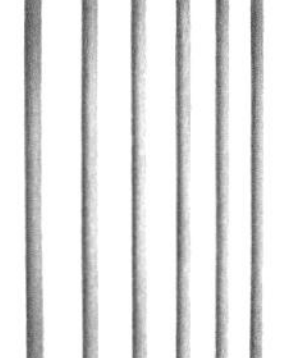

Bullies

Prey or predator—it will be one or the other.

If you are weak, you can be taken advantage of. Maybe it will be desserts handed over, money for the Cantine, maybe clothes, maybe sex.

Brutal, mean, and cruel are words that describe the animal kingdom. It also describes prison life. Without a "car" meaning a group of people that you belong to, a convict is vulnerable.

Gangs are a way of life, even if you are in a prison where known gang members are shipped out to prisons that are better geared to provide higher levels of custody. Gangs are mostly racial—blacks, whites, Hispanics, Pacific Islanders, and a few other but smaller tribes. Sociologists study tribal behavior, and they would only have to spend some time in prison to find a good sample to run a study on.

Race, sex, drugs, and power are the driving forces of prison life. Race is the larger tribe, and being a member of a dominate race brings power, power to get what you want, mostly sex and drugs, but also smaller favors. Old cons will have demands made on them by younger, tougher cons.

The old guys, without backing, can be made into sexual slaves. Is this strong language? I don't think so. The weak, the gang-less, and the tribe-less often become prey.

Every convict that comes into the prison is scouted by other cons to determine their power position. Even the buff, strong looking guys are vulnerable without a gang identity. Sometimes cons will claim an incoming inmate as a sex punk before they even arrive. This is not lost on the administration, and there are segregation cells for those who ask for protection due to one thing or another, but the predators most often, eventually, have their way.

This chapter is titled "Bullies," which is not a prison term, but a contemporary word used in the society at large. Bullies are active in schools, from elementary all the way to college, but mostly among the younger kids. Finding weakness in others is a kid's game. I remember telling bullies even at Woodlawn Grammar School in Portland, Oregon, during the 1940s, "My dad can beat up your dad." In high school I was bullied all the way until my senior year. I know what it is like, and I hate it. When I became a man, I refused to give in to anyone. I will stand up for myself, even if it means getting the crap beat out of me. This attitude has gotten me into a lot of trouble at San Quentin.

While my intolerance to going along to get along is why I survived thirty years as a volunteer at the prison, it also landed me solidly in trouble. I refused to give into the bullies who made demands on me, accused me of racism, and put out death threats against me. Throw me out completely, okay, but I was not going to bend over so I could keep my beige volunteer card.

Someone might ask, "How could a convict bully a volunteer?" Let me count the ways. One, plant a contraband item in a coach's equipment bag. Two, accuse the coach of over-familiarity like groping or something akin to that.

Three, accuse the coach of bringing items in to favored inmates—again, over-familiarity but more serious. Four, have friends on the outside make unwelcome contact with the volunteer. Five, start a rumor campaign designed to defame a coach, which was what happened to me.

This last one may seem less serious than the others, but to me it is not. My reputation is important to me, and I will stand up for it. The trouble is that prison volunteers have little opportunity to address the issues brought up in rumors. The prison officials don't have the time or the obligation to investigate. Often the accusation of a convict will be enough. No appeal, no chance to confront an accuser, no defense at all. The inmates are aware of this and use it to their advantage. Bully all they want, and it rarely results in any discipline.

Most volunteers come into a prison like San Quentin to do some good and are naïve about the dynamics swirling about them. Many quit when they feel the pressure; others are not able to and become foils, the ducks cons love to __uck.

Reality is that there is the good, there is the ugly, and there is the bad.

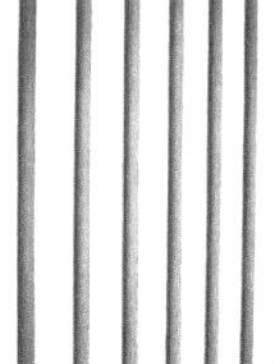

He's Mine, He's Mine!

Twice in my years at San Quentin did I hear shouted out, "He's mine."* And this would have been on a Saturday, these events separated by a year or two, but both times I was there for baseball practice and not for a game.

While down on the baseball field doing whatever, I watched as a bus pulled in on a paved part of the lower yard, the door opened, and out poured guys who had been condemned to prison. I would guess maybe twenty or thirty guys. When the convicts on the lower yard saw the bus, they rushed to get as close as they could to them.

These new arrivals, who were still in their civilian clothing, were about to be handed prison clothes, darkish blue, and all the other stuff they would need like soap, toothbrushes, and so on.

So far, no big deal, but as the new arrivals stepped out of the bus and began heading into the building to their left, the calls began to ring out—"he's mine, he's mine"—as the cons pointed out the guys they were claiming.

"Claiming?"

What do you suppose? Yes, right, claiming the person

as their sexual slave. Maybe *slave* is too harsh and not all together accurate, but you know what I mean.

Well, here you are, youngish, and I would estimate that the majority of the cons were in their twenties and thirties, and no sex! Well, masturbation, but most wanted more.

You had to partner up.

I remember one of our players—he usually played short-stop, and his "partner" would stand behind the dugout, right behind him. I can see him now in my mind's eye—tallish, long light brown hair. I never heard him say a word, but there he was. Usually, the pairing up would not be so obvious, but for some reason…

Was this straight-out homosexuality? I was never able to figure it out. I learned, over the years, that many turned away from a same sex partner when they got out. But now, there is another side to this.

Rape!

Yes, rape. And this in convict's cells, or elsewhere sometimes. I remember the story of a guy who was raped by a male nurse while recovering from surgery in the prison's hospital. (I am still in contact this this man.) And the nurse was not a convict. Have prison guards ever raped a convict? Well, make a wild guess.

Rape—sometimes done as a punishment, perhaps a way to get even, or be sure a person did what he was told to do. A powerful threat indeed.

What can be done about this? is a reasonable question to ask. Over the years I have pressed myself to come up with possible solutions, but I struck out every time. I can come up with a few ideas, but when I analyze these, I usually just give up.

To close out this piece, let me say that if I were in a situation of being made a sexual slave, I would fight as hard as I could to avoid being taken, even if it cost me dearly, in any number of ways. I write this based on what I know about the impact of being made a sexual slave. And this not only for the raped but the raper. Both suffer horribly as a result, often lasting a lifetime. Do not fret, if you disagree with me on this point, but I have to be straight about it.

(*It's mine* will also be heard of in place of He's mine.)

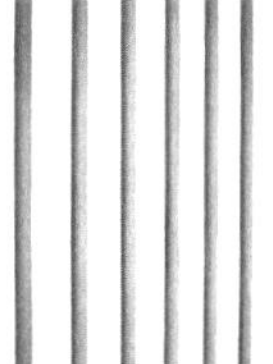

From Elliot Smith

Several years ago I was asked to write a forward for Kent Philpott's book about the 2010 baseball season in San Quentin Prison. I now have the opportunity to discuss a subject that is important to me, which is that people in prison are still human beings whose lives can be changed for the better and they need to treated with humanity and not discarded and thrown in warehouses and forgotten.

For many years I was involved in the baseball program as a player, then a coach and finally the head of the program. I was a volunteer who had a full-time job in San Francisco. I had no special training in prison matters. There were two basic reasons that I chose to get involved with the SQ baseball program and the inmates that participated in the program. First, I wanted to help those inmates associated with the program to make their life in the dark. depressing cell blocks a little better, at least for a few hours, a few days a week, a few weeks each year. Second, I wanted to do as much as I could to help prepare the inmates for the time when they might get out of prison and had to make their way in free society.

Much is written about how difficult it is for inmates to deal with society and day-to-day living once they get out and how difficult it is to stay out. Little is written or understood about how difficult it is to be in prison and be able to do what is necessary to get out.

Whenever I had the chance to address the SQ team for non-baseball matters I would always focus on their need to prepare to get out of prison. My main point was that they had to do whatever it was that was necessary for them to get out and that no matter how old they were when they got out they could have the remainder of their life to experience being out of the darkness where they would have some privacy and the ability to make their own decisions as to such basic things as what to eat and when. One person I knew in SQ was released when he was 70 and later got married and is living a peaceful life.

What follows are my thoughts based on my experience and observations and not scientific studies or reports. The longer I was in the program the more I realized that "doing what was necessary to get out" was easier said than done. There are so many factors bearing down on all the inmates, both personal and institutional, that make it extremely difficult to get out. It seems that there are three ways to get out of the prison system alive: serve the full term, get a parole or get a court order that reverses a conviction or orders a new trial. I will concern myself with the problem of getting a parole or a court order.

As to getting a parole, the California Parole Hearing Process Handbook provides as follows at page 39:

A hearing panel must grant parole at a parole hearing, unless it determines the incarcerated person currently poses an unreasonable risk of danger to society if released from prison. (emphasis added)

The handbook goes on to say the following, quoting

several California Supreme Court cases as authority:

When deciding if a person currently poses an unreasonable risk of danger to society, hearing panels weigh factors relevant to predicting whether the person will commit more antisocial acts, such as crimes of violence, causing personal or financial harm to others, or failing on parole through noncompliance with the reasonable restrictions imposed by their parole agent.

That's it. That's what has to be done to be entitled to a parole. Notice there is nothing stated in the standards necessary to grant a parole about the severity of the crime. The standard is: will the inmate pose an unreasonable risk of danger to society. I will digress a bit. One of the things that irks me the most about discussions regarding paroles is the concept that the original crime is just so serious that the inmate should never be paroled. The inmate's record in prison and the attempts they made to change their life are of no consequence. The fact that all the prison staff evaluating the inmate agree that they are not a danger to society is of no consequence. His original crime is the determining factor, they say. But, murder is murder. It is a heinous, brutal crime. If the original crime is the sole criterion, then no murderer would ever get a parole. They would be doomed to prison without the hope of parole, even though their sentence was not specifically stated as being "without parole".

The absurdity of such a position is best evidenced by the unfortunate case of William Heirens, who at the time of his death was one the longest serving prisoners in the USA, having served 65 years in Illinois. Heirens was convicted of the brutal murder of 6-year old Suzanne Degnan in 1945. The fact that her body parts were stuffed into various sewers in Chicago horrified the public who demanded the murderer be found and convicted. In a frenzy, the police finally decided that Heirens was the murderer and forced his confession after previously forcing a confession from another man, Hector Verburgh, who was later vindicated. (The police said that they were convinced that Verburgh was the killer until he was vindicated.) Heirens was a model prisoner and was one of the first inmates to earn a college degree in prison. He always professed his innocence and said he pleaded guilty to save his life. Basically, everyone knew that Heirens was innocent and the actual killer was known at the time Heirens was convicted. His name was Richard Thomas. An Illinois court even ordered Heirens' release, but because of the seriousness of the crime he was kept in prison by an attorney general and others who had political aspirations and all parole requests were denied.

A second example is someone I knew in SQ. He served 24 years in prison for stealing about $20 worth of groceries, which he did not actually steal. This was a third-strike conviction. His second strike, for which he served his sentence, was of a violent nature. But, to reiterate, he served his punishment for it. He was constantly denied parole for his grocery "theft" because he was a danger to society. Stealing $20 of groceries made him a danger to society worthy of serving 24 years! The real reason for the denials of parole was his second, violent offense. Even though he served his full punishment for that offense, it was used as the reason to deny his parole for his trivial third offense.

So how does an inmate go about showing that they are not a danger to society? One major criterion is that the inmate must take personal responsibility for his crime. In San Quentin, an inmate can take several courses that deal with personal responsibility and anger management. Those inmates serious about getting a parole sign up for these courses and try to better themselves as a result.

Many prisons do not offer the inmates these kind of programs and the inmates have a difficult time dealing with their own personal faults on their own. A player on the baseball team killed a man in a fight that he claimed was self defense because he was attacked. For certain reasons he was denied the ability to make this defense at his trial and he was convicted. He then had to learn to accept the responsibility for his action even though he thought it was justified. This was a long process that was helped by the courses he took and the counseling that was available to him. He finally got to the point where he took full responsibility for his action and did not blame his attacker/victim for his plight.

He posed this problem to me: The cells in SQ are about 9 feet by 4 ½ feet and there is a toilet in the back. The bed is about 6 feet by 3 feet and takes up most of the cell. So, they either sleep with their head next to the bars in the front of the cell or by the toilet in the rear. They choose the front, putting their head right near the corridor where inmates congregate from time to time. His example was that suppose he was not feeling well and tried to sleep but there were people congregating outside his cell talking and making excessive noise. After a while he got up and went into the corridor, and in the most polite and deprecating way asked the people if they could make a little less noise because he didn't feel well and he was trying to sleep. One of the offending inmates pushed him and told him to go fuck himself and things escalated from there. He told me that that would be entirely his fault and not the fault of the inmate who pushed him because he never should have asked them to make less noise in the first place. Had he not gone into the corridor nothing would have happened. Hence, he was at fault. Imagine people in business or daily life on the outside adopting that degree of personal responsibility.

The parole board will probe the inmate to see if they judge their professed assumption of personal responsibility to be genuine. The problem is that a difficult parole board can just use this as a hook to deny parole. That is, they simple find that the inmate has not accepted full responsibility for his actions, since that determination is so subjective.

Another factor in determining if the inmate is a threat to society is if the inmate is sufficiently remorseful for his conduct and can express that remorse in a genuine way. Again the parole board will probe the inmate on this matter to determine their sincerity. But, the same subjectivity exists here, too.

In my experience, many inmates express remorse and admit how immature and stupid they were when they were younger. As an aside, it is a myth that all inmates claim they are innocent. Only a few ever do. Many might say they were over-charged or oversentenced, but not that they were innocent. One inmate that I knew did not tell me for several years that he was innocent because he couldn't trust me enough to tell me until then. He was later exonerated after serving about 27 years. Another inmate, who I realized was innocent, never told me he was innocent. Instead, he took personal responsibility for putting himself in a situation that could become dangerous and could be used against him by the prosecutor. He served about 25 years before getting paroled. In any event, if someone says they are innocent I have learned that you have to at least listen to them.

But, how does someone who is innocent show or express remorse? Are they supposed to show remorse and therefore admit something they did not do? My friend who served 27 years told me he would never go before the parole board and express remorse even if he contrived it. He said he would rather spend the rest of his life in prison than admit to a murder he did not commit and knew nothing about. Had he not obtained a court order after years of work he would still be in prison.

One person I knew on the SQ baseball team was a thief who broke into houses (that he thought were unoccupied at the time) for many years. He thought of these crimes as just property crimes for which the homeowner would have insurance in many cases. But, because of the many courses he was able to take in SQ he realized that the victims suffered mentally after a house robbery in many ways he never imagined. He told me that had he known the degree of pain he caused people he never would have done what he did. He was able to reach that degree of remorse with the aid of the counseling and courses he took in SQ, many of which are not available in many prisons in California and elsewhere.

Because paroles are difficult to get and it takes so many years to get a hearing, many inmates need to get a court order to reverse a perceived injustice in the criminal proceedings. Getting a court order is almost impossible for most inmates who have had some error in their criminal proceedings. Most inmates simply do not have the resources to get a lawyer or legal team to take their case. Some have no family or friends to help them. Many do not have the technical or social skills necessary to reach out to others on the outside. Even the cost of telephoning and mailing to people on the outside is beyond many of the inmates. Some cannot deal with the failure of attempt after attempt and simply give up after a series of frustrating setbacks. One player I knew was serving a life sentence for three strikes. He claimed that the third strike was a frame up and he tried to make his case in court. He became a jailhouse lawyer and helped a lot of other inmates with their legal work. He was working with an outside law firm to try to get a court order to get himself out and did a tremendous amount of research and preparation of briefs and supporting documentation to aid his lawyers. It was extremely difficult for him to get the money necessary for paper, supplies and postage. Finally, after about a year or more he was ready to send his finished product to the law firm. He went to the prison mail room with the proper postage for his package to have it sent off. After quite some time he had not heard from the law firm. They never received his package. Someone in the mail room, either inmate or prison official, threw it out. He had no copy and had to start again.

Even if an inmate has the ability to reach a law firm or agency who helps with appeals and they have the personal character to deal with the frustrations of the process, it is still a difficult proposition. One inmate got a very reputable, but small organization, located in New Jersey, to take his case. It took that organization about 10 years to investigate his case because they were so short-staffed and busy with other cases. They finally hired an investigator and went to the city where the crime was committed to investigate. They cracked the case the first day and got someone to make an admission as to the actual guilty person. It took another 5-6 years to put the case together to be able to get to court to get a hearing on the new evidence they found which included proof that the police fabricated evidence and withheld exonerating evidence. The court found in his favor and ordered his release. But, the local district attorney's office fought him all the way and threatened to retry him.

Finally, it is extremely helpful for an inmate to establish that they are not a threat to society by showing the parole board that they have a full-time job waiting for them when they get out. Otherwise, the thought is that the inmate will just be sitting around waiting to get into trouble again. A job provides the inmate with money, self-respect and a reason to stay out of trouble. But how does an inmate make contact with people from the outside to arrange for a job? It is not easy. The baseball program allowed many people from the outside to be exposed to people on the inside and to realize the people on the inside were not that much different from the people on the outside. In many cases players were able to make contacts who agreed to hire them when they got out. Of course, they had to develop skills inside the prison to make themselves employable. They also had to develop social skills to be able to talk to potential employers on the outside to give confidence to the employer that they could be an asset to their business. The baseball program did serve to improve the social skills of many of the players because of the opportunity to have personal contact. There is a built-in mechanism to break the ice between inmates and free people and that is the common experience and language of baseball. Unfortunately, the opportunities to play on a baseball team only exists in San Quentin and even there only for a few.

Inmates do get out before their sentences terminate. It is not easy, and the prison system appears to make it as difficult as possible to get out. The criteria as stated in the California Parole Hearing Process Handbook look straight-forward and simple to apply, but the road-blocks to get a fair hearing are substantial and in many cases sufficient to frustrate most inmates from obtaining a parole in a timely manner. Inmates lucky enough to be in San Quentin have resources available that are necessary to get out if they are willing to make the supreme effort required. Inmates in other prisons without the same resources find it much more difficult.

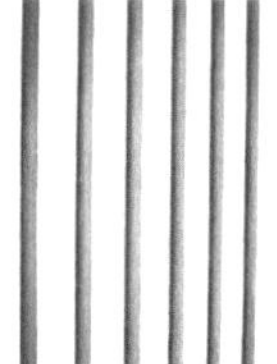

From John Neblett

My name is John Neblett. In 1984 I took the life of Roberto G. After I committed this heinous act, I confessed and pleaded guilty.

In 1997, after having spent the last 12 years of my life in prison, with no end to my imprisonment in sight, I decided to try out for the San Quentin baseball team.

I'd seen the team in action since its reconstitution by Chaplain Smith in 1994. After the disastrous season of 1996, when the team was being coached by the prison's athletic programs director, Coach Denevy, Chaplain Smith and Coach Denevy convinced Kent Philpott to take over.

Kent brought a talented field leader into the program with him, Dan Jones. Together, they proceeded to rebuild a winning club, who, at the time, called themselves the San Quentin Pirates.

I didn't make the team as a starter. Kent and Dan let me stay on as the assistant equipment manager and utility player. This was my role with the club for the next 15 years of my life. Off the field I was the Teacher's aide in the Vocational Electrical Trades Program, then I was the Lead Electrician in the Prison Industries factory.

Through these years Kent taught me many things: first, how to grip a bat with the knuckles of both hands lined up. This was the first step to improving my bat speed. His most important teaching came from acting as a role model. We had our obstacles in the prison. We had the support of the prison administration, but there was active obstruction by staff who took it upon themselves to make it difficult for me to participate. I know the seriousness of my offense, but it was beyond their imagination to see I deserved anything other than being punished for still existing.

But Kent was there to hear me, and his patience and focus on the mission of making our program happen taught me to appreciate the prison staff who were supportive and professional in spite of the opposition of their peers.

I paroled on August 15, 2015 after having spent 30 years inside. Kent had me in his home Christmas day for dinner. He would have provided anything I needed had I needed anything, seeing him since, and remembering being his guest that day brings me tears of joy.

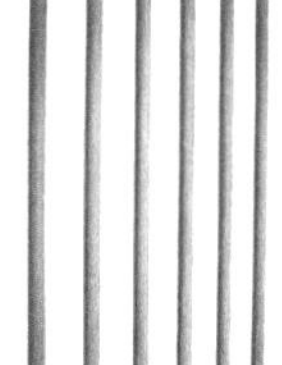

Letter for J. Neblett

January 26, 2015

Board of Prison Terms

Re. John O. Neblett D-04841
San Quentin State Prison,

I have known John for about 20 years now. I was the baseball coach there at San Quentin from 1997 to 2012 and John played on the team but mostly he was equipment manager. The program, and this may seem like a stretch, but the program would not have been the same without the hard work and faithfulness of John Neblett.

Over the years we have spoken many dozens of times, which allowed me to get to know him quite well. The change of attitude about who he was and what had landed him in prison was observable. He became one of the few convicts I learned I could trust to tell me the truth and never once did he attempt to make me break the rules or influence me to do that which we all knew was against the law.

John has been in prison a long while, has taken advantage of so many different programs. He has grown a lot, into a mature man.

You would be able to make a sound judgment about John simply on the basis of knowing who his friends are. These individuals are persons of substance, realible people, both free and not. Also, John has earned the respect of prison staff, both in the education department but also in the Protestant chapel. My son, Vernon, who for years ran the flag football program, thinks of lot of John as well. We both would welcome him as a neighbor.

Sincerely,

Kent Philpott, Sr. Pastor
Miller Avenue Church
Mill Valley, CA

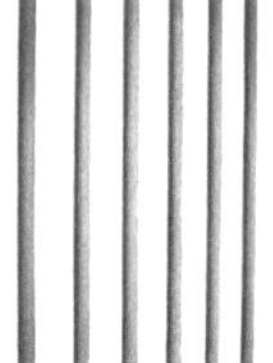

From Kevin Loughlin

My five-year tenure as a coach and manager for San Quentin Giants from 2012 to 2017 was one of the greatest experiences of my life. It started off as a huge challenge with a lot of doubt and trepidation. It ended with building some fabulous relationships and watching the positive growth of these men. Truely one of the most rewarding times of my life.

My story at San Quentin Prison began with playing Little League baseball just outside the prison grounds as a 12-year-old Little League player in the late1960s. You had to enter the prison grounds through the intimidating 20-foot black metal gate to get to the baseball field. Those entering had to open your trunk going in and out of the prison for obvious reasons. Imagine that today playing Little League in that environment? The ironic part was this drive on the grounds of this notorious prison led to the most beautiful Little League field you've ever seen.

I would have the opportunity to coach some of the same inmates who umpired and manicured our beautiful Field of Dreams!

After a fairly successful High School career, I gave

some thought about playing college ball down in San Diego, but instead fell in love with the beach. In my 3rd year at SDSU, I needed an extra class, so I took a criminology class where one of the guest speakers was an inmate from San Quentin prison. It turns out that he was incarcerated there while I played little baseball at San Quentin.

He gave a fascinating overview of prison life. It was very intimating place but there was a beacon of light at the end of the tunnel with his release. I asked a simple question about what the policy for family visits was and stated my name Kevin Loughlin.

At that point his weathered yet joyful face lit up, and he repeated my name. Turns out when you hit a home run at San Quentin Little League the inmates would stencil your name up on the left field cement wall. I was lucky enough to hit a few home runs there, but the fact that he would remember my name ten years after I played a Little League at the Q was one of the most rewarding moments of my life.

Because of these great memories, I felt like I wanted to give back to these very individuals who had served time and eventually and hoped to be released. I initially started playing on men's team that played against the SQ Giants. The resounding sound of the metal doors closing behind you after walking through a metal detector is a sound I will never forget as we walked down to the baseball field.

The long walk down the runway to the field surrounded by hundreds of inmates was a sight few people experience. This was no field of dreams, but then again it was their Yankee Stadium no matter the poor condition of this dirt field.

Those with good behavior were able to try out for the team and the talent ranged from not very good to some of them possibly being able to play D1 or D2 college ball if they had not been incarcerated.

The most difficult thing following these first two weeks was having to tell numerous young men that they had not made the team. The tears in their eyes told the story of how much emotion was involved and how badly they wanted to play for the San Quentin Giants. This was after all the most prestigious team within the prison walls of San Quentin and an honor to be selected.

One of the requirements after a background check to coach was signing an agreement not to patronize with these men for obvious reasons.

However, after spending two days a week and six to eight hours a week with these individuals there is no way I could not take an interest in these men. Just like the out-side world, each inmate had their own unique personality, some were dangerous, some couldn't be trusted but many of these men were led by their hearts. All were deter-mined to work hard and give themselves a few hours to feel somewhat free.

Every man that came out to the field for a two-hour practice or a three-hour game, walked down the long stair-case to the field with a smile on their face and a smile when they left. The difference is we got to leave while they enter their 8x12 foot cells every single day and in some cases a lifetime.

Our teams were competitive, we overachieved and that's all we could ask for from these determined ball play-ers. The greatest satisfaction was knowing that close to three quarters of these inmates have been released and are now out in the world making new lives for themselves

I keep in touch with many of the members of the team. They were so grateful for someone to volunteer their time and give them a few hours of peace and tranquility in con-trast to the reality of life in prison.

I feel truly blessed to have shared a small part of my life with the guys at the Q. There isn't a day that goes by that I don't think of this life-changing experience that I had with San Quentin baseball.

Good luck Men and here's to the San Quentin Giants!

Coach
Kevin Loughlin

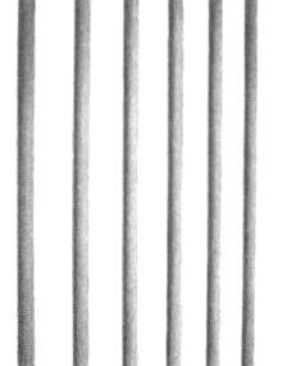

From Len Zemarkowits

San Quentin Baseball - A Volunteer's Perspective

Whether it was serendipity or the stars being in the proper alignment, my experience with the baseball program at San Quentin began with a chance meeting with the author of this book, Kent Philpott.

After coaching various baseball programs, I accepted a position

as the junior varsity baseball coach at a local Marin County high school.

During practices I was introduced to Kent who was the freshman coach. We discussed various baseball philosophies and practice techniques when we crossed paths. One afternoon on the field Kent asked me if I would like to play baseball. Not having played for many years, I thought it might be fun. I said, "Sure, where do we play ?"

The answer: San Quentin. "Are you crazy," I replied. "I am going to play inside a prison? " Kent assured me it would be a worthwhile experience so I agreed.

The process to be admitted to San Quentin is a bit cumbersome and time consuming. After submitting a driver's license and social security number, a background check is conducted. Any prior felonies prevents admittance to the prison. After several weeks clearance was obtained and our team was allowed in.

Arriving and getting into San Quentin is the next part of the saga. Last Marin County exit, San Quentin, the sign read. If missed, you end up on the bridge headed to Richmond. The road to the east gate is a narrow two lane road with old, well kept bungalow homes on either side. The views of the San Francisco Bay are magnificent.

After parking in the visitors' lot, we assembled at the east gate where the usual, not too cheerful corrections officer made sure we were on the approved list and properly attired. No denim! No jeans! As I soon learned, the inmates wear denim and you do NOT want to be considered an inmate. I mistakenly showed up in jeans once and was denied admission.

The games versus the inmates were fun although mostly forgettable. I do recall being picked off third base by the catcher while I was lollygagging off third base. I realized these guys meant business.

Playing conditions could be an issue. While playing left field, with a high overcast, it was difficult to pick up a batted ball. The background being a dirty beige 25 foot high wall with rifle toting guards atop it. The ball seemed to disappear.

I do not recall if it was the same season or the following, but Kent asked me to help coach the San Quentin Giants. Based on my interactions with the players, I accepted.

Now I had to become a volunteer, not a one day visitor. The prison regulations required volunteers to be "Brown Card" holders. The Brown Cards were kept at the East Gate Guard Shack and necessary to be admitted and to accompany visiting baseball teams. This process was under the watchful eye of the aforementioned not so cheerful officer.

Brown Card training required a two hour class in a meeting room outside of the prison walls. Higher level corrections officers taught the class and tried to prepare us for the experience at San Quentin.

Volunteers were not only involved in baseball.

San Quentin offers many programs, including music, art, theater (Shakespeare anyone ?), High School equivalency diplomas, two year and four year college degrees. Many undergraduates from UC Berkeley taught classes. Other sports include tennis, basketball, flag football, soccer and long distance running.

Without question the most important issue for volunteers is safety and the primary safety tool is a whistle. All volunteers are required to wear one. A blast of the whistle resulted in an immediate response from the corrections officers.

After several hours of important do's and don't's, we had to compete a state form with a great deal of personal information for a background check. My favorite question: "Are you blind?" It occurred to me that if I was I would not be able to read the question. Being an umpire as well as a coach, I had been asked that question more than once.

Nothing quite prepares a volunteer for the first visit inside of San Quentin. After signing in and obtaining the brown card, it is a several hundred yard walk to the main entrance.

At the entrance the brown card is shown again along with another signature. Next is the Sally Port. This is a series of two barred gates electronically controlled by an officer behind a thick glass barrier. The first gate opens, a number of us enter and the gate behind us is closed and locked. GULP. We show our brown cards again and the interior gate is opened.

Welcome to San Quentin. The first impression of San

Quentin is almost like a step back in time. It is reminiscent of a medieval fortress. The place is old! It opened in July, 1852. The original hospital, facing the courtyard, was built in 1885. The façade still exists but the old hospital was replaced with a modern facility.

Through the courtyard , down a small paved road, and here is the yard. The baseball field dominates the view but additionally there are tennis and basketball courts. Surrounding the field, high prison walls, guard towers and walk ways, and a fence topped with razor wire. The infield is all dirt and the outfield is worn chopped up grass. The players do take pride in the field and maintain it as well as possible. They rake and line the infield when chalk is available, and water down the field if is the plumbing is cooperating that day. Canada geese regularly visit to eat what little vegetation exists and leave their droppings everywhere. The players use rakes and remove as much of the "presents" as they can.

One other remarkable feature of the San Quentin baseball field is the razor wire on top of the outfield fence. Needless to say, caution is required when trying to rob a potential home run. Many soccer balls have met an inglorious end at the top of the fence.

The following season Kent asked me if I would manage the other San Quentin baseball team, the San Quentin A's. In addition to the A's being my favorite team, I thought it would be an interesting challenge to manage a baseball team under rather unique circumstances.

The chance to be on one of the San Quentin baseball teams is met with an overwhelming response from the inmates. We only had about 18 to 20 spots per team and the demand was many times greater. Tryouts were tense.

To me, the most difficult part of coaching, whether high school or at San Quentin, is telling a player they did not make the team. Feelings are raw and any explanation does not suffice. Respect is an important issue. Not making the team is perceived as being disrespected. Not a pleasant situation.

An inmate, a former player, was my assistant coach, and he helped me navigate the culture at San Quentin. He also had insight as to which guys would be good teammates or who would be troublemakers.

Developing talent is the crux of coaching. Honing players skills, bringing out their potential, is the goal of a coach. Trying to find practice time was difficult at best. Usually I would try to have practice on a weekday afternoon after "The Count."

From what I understand, inmates throughout the California Prison System are counted several times a day. If the numbers do not add up the prison goes into lockdown. No one is allowed out of their cells. One of my most harrowing experiences occurred on an afternoon when we had a practice scheduled and the count failed.

I arrived about 4:30 pm at the East Gate and went through the usual process. The officer at the gate said I could enter in spite of the situation. After passing the checkpoints, I went down to the baseball field and sat in the dugout. There was nobody in the yard and the place was deathly quiet. I thought, " What would it be like if I was going to be here for the next 5, 10, or 20 years ?" There is not much to see. A glimpse of the West Marin hills at best. Would I kill myself, would I go insane ? Fortunately, after about 45 minutes the all clear was given and the players came down to the field. I did not have to make either of those unpleasant choices.

While on the topic of being "inside", I recall one of the players saying to me, "Coach, if you ever go to prison make sure you come here to San Quentin." After a good laugh, I told him I think I would stay with Plan B.

On other occasions, for whatever reason, we were not allowed in at the usual time. A visiting team, including Bill "Spaceman" Lee were waiting at the East Gate. Bill Lee, a former major league pitcher, regaled us with stories from his MLB days. One particular story stands out. Bill said, " When I played for the Washington Senators Ted Williams managed the team. (1969-1971). Everyone always talked about what a great hitter Ted was. He was a good hitter alright ! He was always hitting on my wife." Even in is 60's, it was amazing to watch Bill pitch. A curveball that fell off the table and an incredible pick-off move.

During the season baseball teams from around the San Francisco Bay area came to San Quentin to play. One team from the Los Angeles area showed up every spring. If I remember correctly they played both Saturday and Sunday as they had traveled such a long distance. This group was very generous. As the baseball program had very little to no funding equipment was at a premium. This LA team would donate 5 dozen balls at a minimum. Bats and gloves were also donated. To say we were grateful would be an understatement.

On the topic of visiting teams, a tip of the cap to Kent Philpott who worked his butt off to bring teams in to play.

Back to coaching: The old joke about the tourist who stops a New Yorker and asks, "How do you get to Carnegie Hall?" The New Yorker replies, "Practice, Practice, Practice." The same applies to baseball. Baseball is a game of failure. In case this idea is forgotten there is reminder on the scoreboard: Runs, Hits, ERRORS. There is no other pursuit in life that 3 out of 10 results in fame and fortune. Of course, in the background, the baseball gods (lower case) are ready to humble anyone who gets too puffed up.

We had practice whenever the schedule would allow. With two San Quentin teams field time was limited. Rather than bore the reader with minutiae, I tried to teach fundamentals to the team. I relied on Dusty Baker's hitting techniques, Tom House for pitching and a batting Tee. As much as the players disliked the Tee it helped correct upper cutting specifically. I called it "Mr. T" after the character in the old TV show. If you think it is easy to hit a stationary ball without hitting the tee, try it.

Playing baseball inside San Quentin is a unique experience with a long history. I found on the Central Pacific Railroad Photographic History Museum website pictures of a baseball program from July 24, 1932. Listed are the players from Southern Pacific, first and last name and position. The San Quentin All Stars listed by last name only. The score was not noted.

Perhaps the most unusual feature of San Quentin baseball, aside from razor wire, high prison walls, and guards with rifles, was the dreaded "alarm." At any moment, whether during a game, during practice, or just walking to the field, an alarm might sound. The alarm meant something in violation of the prison rules had happened. A tone would sound followed by an announcement, "Down in the yard." At this point all the inmates had to sit or "take a knee' wherever they were. Not adhering to this protocol had very serious consequences. Usually the alarms were resolved quickly. However, many times they seemed to go on and on.

Game days, usually on Saturdays, when a visiting team came to play, were exciting. The attitude of the players was different as this was their time to shine. The game was a big draw with the yard population. Seating around the backstop was at a premium. Having umpired as well as coached, I can attest to the commentary being some of the funniest I have ever heard.

The change in the players prior to a game was almost palpable. As mentioned earlier, the inmates all wore the mandatory blue denim jackets and pants. On the back and down one leg was printed, CDC Prisoner." CDC meaning California Department of Corrections. Now they were allowed to morph from prisoners into baseball players. One could see them swell with pride.

The games were hotly contested with stats and bragging rights on the line. Stats were kept from game to game and season to season. Games between the "home teams", A's and Giants, occasionally got a little chippy. Best behavior was displayed when a visiting team came to play. I can only recall one incident between the A's and Giants that resulted in both teams being sent to their respective dugouts. A "Do you want to play baseball ?" lecture followed delivered by yours truly. Cooler heads prevailed.

I am going to conclude a couple of stories. After a practice or a game and the leaving the prison, I was aware of two sentiments. One was that I was able to walk out of San Quentin and go home. Secondly was the feeling of exhilaration. This emotion evolved from the thought that I might have helped someone. For the guys stuck inside, learning and playing baseball might have brought them some happiness and self respect.

Near the end of my time coaching the San Quentin A's, there was a young man who was new to the team. He was quiet, reserved and a decent ballplayer. As I got to know him he told me he was incarcerated due to an addiction to opioids. After a game or practice, I do not recall, he said to me, "Coach, you know these two hours are two hours that I am not in prison."

With all the years of coaching at San Quentin that one sentence made it all worthwhile.

Len Zemarkowitz

Len's Baseballs

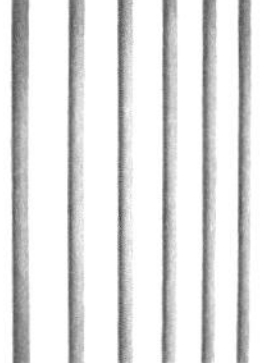

4: A Plea

"Post Traumatic Stress Disorder"—Does this have any-thing to do with the subject of this book?

I think it may. Trauma—injury that is mostly emo-tional—starts finding us early on. We are often unaware of its presence. Undetected it worms its way into our inner being and hacks us to pieces.

Mostly we think of PTSD as something that happens to war veterans. Many of the men and women coming back from Iraq and Afghanistan have it. I wrote a book about an Army Ranger who fought in the Vietnam War called, Recollections of a Warrior, who to this day struggles with it though he has made significant progress. My son Vernon fought in the first Gulf War, named Desert Storm, and we have talked about whether he has been impacted by it as well.

Since 1986 I have led a workshop for those who have lost relationships, mainly due to divorce, and I have won-dered if some of them have experienced trauma to the point that they might have developed PTSD.

This may be taking it too far, or maybe not, others will have to judge, but I think many in our society have been traumatized by doing nothing more than growing up in a toxic and dangerous culture. With the anger, the fear, the rejection, poor health, poor education, poor parenting—and the list goes on—could a diagnosis of PTSD be appropriate for more people than thought at this point? But more to the point, does being in prison constitute trauma? And I am not referring only to the prisoners.

I wonder about myself. I wonder if I might not have touches of it, too. Correctional officers are definitely vulnerable. Teachers, medical workers, clerical staff, people in the upper echelons like wardens—yes, they are also living in a hostile and toxic environment. Convicts without a doubt are exposed to mental tortures, most unintentionally inflicted, but there nevertheless. There is a certain hopelessness implied in what I am saying here, and I have no blame to place on anyone. It is simply the nature of the beast.

My purpose here is to call attention to the issue for both prisoners and their keepers. It is probably not sensible to think that we act as our brothers' keepers across the board since, it would mean prisoners having some graciousness, if not merely understandings of the problems the prison officials face. To envision grace being extended to prisoners by prison staff—is that crazy? I am not meaning ignoring the need to keep prisoners in prison and to protect the public at large from the worst among us.

I have witnessed prisoners treating officers with respect and honor. Not often, but I have seen it. And I have even more often seen prison staff treating convicts with respect and honor. PTSD—more will be revealed—but having a degree of empathy for each other may be (just?) out of the realm of possibility.

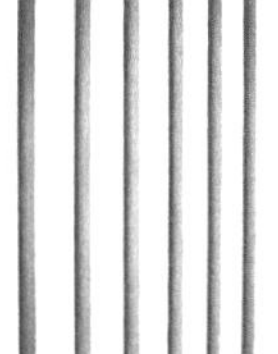

A Former Prison Guard Tells His Story

How did an upper middle-class white boy become a guard at San Quentin Prison?

If you're an inmate—or were one—you might think we'd have nothing in common. I used to think this way when I viewed the world through the lens of right and wrong and black and white. I came into San Quentin not as a prisoner, but as a correctional officer—armed with assumptions, biases, and a blind confidence in my own world view. But the prison didn't just teach me about others. It forced me to confront everything I thought I knew about myself.

What surprised me most wasn't the violence or the rigid routine—it was the humanity I found in a place that supposedly stripped it away. Men who'd been written off by society became mirrors in which I saw parts of myself. In ways I never expected, I realized that I had more in common with these inmates than I did with the people I grew up around.

I was raised in a small town, the kind where appearances mattered and imperfections were hidden behind manicured lawns. On paper, my childhood was the textbook version of stability: upper-middle-class, two parents, a nice home. But beneath the surface, things were brittle. My father, a respected dentist, had little interest in parenting. He was emotionally distant—resentful, even of the obligations that came with being a husband and father. My mother shined at dinner parties and social events, but at home, she seemed like a ghost. She chased admiration, not connection.

We—my two sisters and I—were left to raise ourselves in a house filled with things but empty of presence. I had freedom, yes, but it came with a quiet abandonment. No one taught me how to understand my emotions, how to relate to others, or how to navigate the messiness of life. I grew up as an observer, always watching from the outside, never really feeling like I belonged anywhere.

That outsider feeling followed me into adulthood. I didn't join SQ for the power, the badge, or the routine. I just needed a job. If I'm honest, I wasn't sure why I was there. But those eight months inside became a kind of unintentional pilgrimage—one that stripped away my illusions of what I thought the words right and wrong meant. This forced me to reckon with the life I'd lived and the person I was becoming.

At San Quentin, I encountered lives far different from mine on the surface, but under the skin, I recognized the same wounds—neglect, disconnection, longing. I stopped judging and started listening. For the first time, I felt I was learning about myself.

I'm writing down some of the moments that shaped me during those months. Not because they're extraordinary, but because they changed me in ways I never expected. These aren't just prison stories—they're human stories.

My Time at San Quentin

I was hired without much fanfare at SQ. Before I knew it, I was enrolled in a one-month Correctional Officers Academy, surrounded by men and women of all ethnicities.

Most of the new recruits were older men, recently retired from the military. They called it "double-dipping"—drawing a military pension while starting a second career in corrections. The Veterans Transition Program encouraged this, pitching prison work as a seamless next step for seasoned veterans. I was 25, among the youngest in the group. These veterans —grey-haired and stoic—seemed weathered by life. San Quentin already fit them like a well-worn glove.

On the first day of the academy, an older prison guard (had he been at SQ for years or was he one of the veterans?) led 30 new recruits on a tour of the facility. Without a word of warning, the old guard took us into the heart of the prison. As we turned a corner, the stark red brick of the exterior gave way to worn, grey-cement painted blocks inside—surfaces that had been layered over again and again with grey paint, each coat attempting to mask decades of use and decay.

As we rounded the next corner in the prison the walls narrowed, forcing us to walk closer together as the old guard quickened his walking pace. The industrial fluorescent lighting was dim and flickered at us as we approached.

Then came the shock. Dozens of faces pushed up against dimly lit prison bars, staring at us.

Then a crush of inmates behind the ones with faces already against the bars surged toward the bars, just four feet from where we stood. The once dim quiet setting was now echoing barks and yells, jeers and catcalls like a pack of caged animals.

"He's cute!"

"Look at the butt on that one!"

"Ooowww—I'm gonna make that one my girlfriend."

"His lips are so pretty."

We all gave a gasp and froze for a moment. We didn't laugh or curse—just a quick involuntary stare into to the eyes of men who live behind bars. I looked over at the old guard. There was a gleam in his eyes, a smirk on his face. He was loving every second of this, and he stopped for about 20 seconds in front of the inmates. It seemed longer. Suddenly the old guard started walking again and we followed gladly behind him. Later when I thought about that incident It felt like it was a hazing ritual passed down from guard to guard over the decades. San Quentin opened in 1852.

We passed into another wing—silence, inmate-free—the guard's tone shifted. Stern, belittling.

"Alright. Who wants to quit now? Because this—this is your job, day in and day out. It only gets worse from here. So, if you're going to quit, do it now and stop wasting everyone's time."

A heavy silence followed. No one moved. We just stood there trying to make sense of what we had just witnessed.

Then it clicked—this had been staged for our benefit. A play put on by the old guard and the inmates just for us.

A scare tactic meant to weed out the weak and give the old guards a laugh while giving the prisoners a distraction from the daily routine of boredom.

After we (the new recruits) were released for the day, I drove back to my studio apartment that was six times as large as a cell in SQ. I had comparison now. Noticing the painted whiteish walls with used older mostly working appliances and in the background the sound of a siren just like any city anywhere in America.

I needed a job and SQ was offering me one with no previous experience required, they said. I was a perfect fit with no experience at much of anything. I'll take it.

When you finally graduate from the academy you are now a certified correctional officer. The prison administration wants to find out where you fit the prison best. The first 2 months you are assigned to different parts of the prison. Every week a new position—mess hall, yard, gym, laundry, visiting room, tower or wall duty carrying a gun.

My First Post at San Quentin—A Test of Nerve

My first assignment at San Quentin was in the mess hall—a place where the general population gathered 3 times a day for meals. It was a stage where an undercurrent of boredom and violence existed just below the surface, constrained and accepted by everyone who works or lives at SQ. Where order was quick to unravel.

If you ever find yourself in the mess hall in SQ, look up at the celling. The ceiling is 3 stories, 25 feet high. If you look carefully, you'll notice hundreds of metal forks in the stucco ceiling. Ever try to lodge something in a ceiling 25 feet from the ground? This was my favorite image I keep in my mind when talking about SQ. Not the gas chamber or the front tower as you enter, that has a view of the whole yard entrance. This tower with windows that slide so as to allow a machine gun (They keep locked behind steel doors) mounts onto a turret with a view of the whole yard.

The mess hall Sergeant, wearing "seen it all before" demeaner was waiting for me at the office door at the back of the mess hall. He was stern and to the point: "You're here to keep the peace," he said. "Make sure the line moves, "no one takes more than they are allowed"- the sergeant pointed to a prepared plate of food for me to see. I thought to myself that seems like a good amount of food. I nodded, He continued, "It is of the upmost importance that the food does not run." The sergeant looked at me with a steady gaze now and emphasized: if each inmate takes more than his share the food will run out. Then he spoke with a lower tone as to not draw attention to his words: *"The mess hall is where trouble starts."* He gestured to the catwalk above where four armed officers stood watch. "They are there if you need them. Do your job." With that, he disappeared into his office. I wouldn't see him again until the end of my shift.

I walked out to the mess hall already full of inmates lining up for breakfast. Just a note-All of the people who work in the mess hall are inmates, too, except for the head chef. The first breakfast rush had started -so I thought I guess I am ready.

At first, everything moved smoothly. The line of inmates shuffled along, and I started to feel like I had a handle on things. But near the end of the line, I noticed someone didn't fit the flow. One inmate—massive, easily 6'6", all muscle—was walking slowly, visibly sweating, twitching, looking angry, eyes wild. As he neared the food stations, he began piling food onto his tray—far more than the rules allowed.

I froze, unsure how to respond. My mind was racing. Was he on something? Was he about to go psychotic?

As I focused on this inmate, something in the room shifted. I quickly scanned the dining area maybe hoping for some help.

What I did notice was all the inmates had stopped eating. All the inmate eyes were on me. Some were smirking. Others were laughing as they watched.

That's when it hit me: This was a setup.

A test.

They wanted to see how the new guy would respond.

Would I cave and allow this big scary inmate to take whatever he wanted?

Would I stand firm and if I did what could I do to stop him?

In that instant, I realized this moment would define my time at San Quentin. If I let this go, if I gave in to intimidation on Day One, I'd be marked. They'd know I could be pushed around. It would never stop.

Before I knew it, the inmate, the 6'6" giant, stood next to me. His tray messy and overflowing. Up close, I could see he was dripping sweat, breathing heavy and fast, muscles tense. His eyes locked on mine. He didn't say a word. He didn't have to. His body was daring me to act. The whole mess hall grew quiet.

This was the moment I knew I should act. But I was not sure what was going to do.

What was I going to do? This was still a question in my mind.

My body tensed. But almost without my permission my arm suddenly moved forward as if someone else was moving it. I grabbed his forearm and with all my strength and pulled him out the chow line.

I expected a violent reaction-maybe a punch or an attack.

Was I wrong about this being a test? I was scared.

To my great relief, this big inmate relaxed his body. His face became calm. He spoke to me in a soft childlike voice "What's wrong officer?" he said with a hint of a smile on his face.

"You've taken too much food." Trying to use my adult scolding voice that cracked as I said these words.

The inmate looked at me and then at his tray and said with a knowing smile. "I wasn't paying attention. I am sorry." I took his tray of food and asked him to get back in line with a new tray.

The whole mess hall at that moment came back to life. Somehow, I sensed that maybe they were all a little disappointed. Strangely, the 4 guards on the wall seemed a little disappointed as well.

I was proud of myself. Yet no one at SQ mentioned it. Not the guards on the wall. Not the inmates in the mess hall.

I guess this was just another day in SQ.

That evening, after the dinner feeding was over, my job was to make sure that none of the dozen inmates who worked in the mess hall had taken any knives, forks, or spoons with them. Each inmate did have a brown paper bag they carried. Curious, I stopped the first inmate walking out of the mess hall with his bag and asked if I could see what was inside. I opened the bag to find bread, fruit, and lunch meat.

I told the inmate, "Sorry, you can't take this out of the mess hall."

The inmate told me that the other guard let them.

I said, "Sorry," and took his bag. Then all the other inmates filed by and left their bags with me as well. I was pleased—I showed them who was in charge and that I was not to be taken advantage of. I was new, but not naïve, I thought to myself.

The next morning, I was in the mess hall at 5 a.m. to start my shift, expecting the inmates to arrive around the same time. It was now 5:15 a.m., and not one inmate had arrived to start prepping the food. I asked the Chef "Where are the inmates?"

The Chef just shrugged and said, "Tell your sergeant no one's here yet."

I walked to the sergeant's office and knocked. The sergeant opened the door and came out, clearly annoyed that

I was bothering him.

I spoke up, "Sergeant, none of the inmates have shown up for work today." My expression was perplexed and puzzled.

The sergeant's eyes opened wide. With a quick glance around the room to confirm that no inmates were in the mess hall, he shouted at me from two feet away, "Go to their cells and ask them why they are not working today… Go now! You have 15 minutes to fix this!"

As I was walking away, I turned around and said, with a little desperation in my voice, "What if they won't come to work?"

The sergeant looked across at me with anger in his voice. "You do whatever you have to do to get them back to work!"

As I walked out toward the inmates' cells, I thought, *Whatever I have to? Maybe I should get more guards and force them to work? What else could I do? Then I thought, Let me talk to them before I do anything else.*

I approached their cells, and the group who worked in the mess hall was waiting for me. I calmly asked them, "Why are you not at work today?"

One of the older inmates, who seemed to be the leader of the group, nonchalantly replied, "Because, Officer, you're not allowing us to take food back to our cells. We don't work for the fun of it—we work to get food so we can sell it back in the cell blocks."

I suddenly realized what the sergeant meant by *Do whatever you have to do to get them back to work.* The sergeant knew I needed to strike a deal with the inmates about food. The inmates knew this too, and I had to learn it the hard way. The deal I struck with them was without the sergeant's blessing, and if it was ever discovered, it would fall solely on me.

Time was running out to get the inmates back to work. I agreed, but I said, "I want to look in your bags each night to make sure you're not taking too much."

The inmates all agreed, and as if it had been planned (and I believe it was), they were all ready and hurried to the mess hall.

That night, as they left the mess hall, I looked in each of their bags and removed half the food they had placed inside. There was a lot of grumbling as I did this. I thought I was being more than fair.

I was reassigned that night. Instead of a week, I was reassigned after only two days.

The Laundry—my new assignment

The Laundry is the most isolated place in SQ, as my new Laundry Sergeant informed me. He said the laundry is one of the best places to kill someone without being seen. The inmates know this as well. Guards don't have to worry about being assaulted by inmates in most cases. Guards are seldom attacked because of the consequences for such actions. The consequence the inmates fear most is not prison time—but something much more deadly: SQ gang leaders.

Why? If a guard is assaulted, the prison goes into lockdown for weeks as the incident is investigated. No visiting is allowed during lockdown. Visiting from family and friends is cherished by inmates. Everything happens in the visiting hall. It's a crowded room full of kids and wives, sex and drugs. You can't write an inmate up unless you see naked genitals. You can see sex acts going on, but unless you see genitals, he cannot be written up. The consequence for the inmate who commits an assault on a guard and causes all inmates to lose visiting rights is usually death.

As I entered the Laundry, I noticed that unlike most of

SQ—which is open and easy to navigate—the Laundry is a maze of corridors and enclosed rooms filled with noisy washing machines and dryers constantly running. The noise would easily muffle any cries for help or pain. (This is how I thought of the Laundry.) I saw room after room with no one inside, machines whirling and loud. I finally made it to a room with the large industrial washing machines, and inside was one inmate—a big man, 6'4" and all muscle. When I looked at his face, I noticed his eyes. They looked gentle—not fierce, as I had expected.

I introduced myself and reached out to shake his hand. It was an awkward moment, as our handshakes revealed different cultural upbringings—mine was the standard hand thrust with the thumb up, and his was a clasp with fingers interlocking mine.

"Hi," the inmate said. "People here call me Bone Crusher."

Over the week I spent in the Laundry, Bone Crusher and I talked to pass the hours. He slowly revealed to me that he was muscle for a gang called The Black Gorilla Family. He had spent most of his life—from a troubled kid to now a 31-year-old adult—in the prison system. He said, with a truthful, calm confession in his voice, "I prefer being inside and not on the streets."

By the time my week as the laundry guard was over, Bone Crusher and I had developed a friendly understanding. Whenever we passed each other in the yard or the cell block, we said hello.

My stay in the laundry position lasted 7 days, then I was reassigned.

Death Row—reassignment #3

My next week's assignment was on Death Row. The name itself gave me chills. I made my way up to Death Row early

Monday morning, climbing stairs to enter a large room. Half the room was filled with cells, and I was surprised by the fresh breeze coming off the bay through the large open windows on the wall opposite the cells, about 40 yards away. I thought, *That seems like an invitation to escape,* there were no guards with guns in sight. It was just me and my new sergeant, who barely said a word to me. He pointed to the cells and said, "Your post is over there by the floor-to-ceiling wire fence." (The type of fence you'd expected to see at a construction site.)

I walked over to my spot, which allowed me to see all the Death Row cells. I arrived at my post and noticed there was another floor-to-ceiling fence with heavier gauge wire about 15 yards in front of me. I felt better that there was a second fence between me and the inmates. Then, about 10 more yards beyond that, were the Death Row cells. Each cell was open-faced with heavy bars. The cement walls and floors were painted with grey paint. This part of SQ looks old, it had been there since the prison opened in 1852. The whole building felt old and tired.

I stood at my post where all the Death Row inmates could see me—and more importantly, where I could see them. None of the inmates seemed to even notice I was there; they completely ignored me. After about an hour went by, I kept staring into each individual cell, trying to determine if they were planning an escape. The cells were about 40 yards away, and nothing seemed amiss. But I thought, *They must be planning something* (I'd watched too many movies)—but it wasn't going to happen while I was on duty.

Suddenly, my concentration was broken by a Death Row inmate yelling something. I listened, trying to figure out which cell this inmate was yelling too—and why he was yelling.

He shouted again, "Hey, you asshole! Throw me some matches, asshole!"

I noticed the inmate was pointing directly at me, arm stretched out, finger aimed. "Yes! You, asshole! Throw me some matches!"

My eyes followed his finger I now saw there were about 20 packs of matches hanging on the fence I stood by, about 20 feet away. I looked at the matches, then back at the inmate, and he yelled again more impatient: "Asshole, I said throw me some fucking matches!"

I looked over to him and finally said, "No. Not if you're going to call me names. Say please."

I thought, *I will show him who's in control around here.*

But to my surprise, the Death Row inmate yelled at the top of his lungs, "Sergeant! Sergeant! ...Sergeant!!"

I laughed to myself. That won't work. The sergeant will just ignore him.

But to my surprise, the sergeant burst out of his office with an angry look in his eyes.

That inmate's going to get a tongue-lashing now, I thought. I stood there proudly, pleased with myself. *The sergeant will be proud of me for demanding respect from these inmates.*

The sergeant yelled, "What!?" to the Death Row inmate.

"That asshole won't throw me any matches!" the inmate shouted, pointing at me.

Good, I thought. *He used the word 'asshole' in front of the sergeant.*

But the sergeant suddenly turned toward me and, looking me directly in the eye, said loudly and clearly:

"Give him some matches."

I was taken aback. Hadn't he heard that this inmate called me an asshole?

"Sergeant," I said, "he called me an asshole."

The sergeant, walking back toward his office with an annoyed expression, looked back at me and said:

"If you can't take someone calling you an asshole—or any other word—this is not the place for you."

With that, he turned his back and disappeared into his office for the rest of the day.

My stay in the death row position lasted 1 day. I was reassigned.

In the next 7 months at San Quentin there were many lessons to learn about myself and other people and inmates. About a system that runs despite itself. About guards that must learn to bend but not cross over the line, and about inmates who learn to work within a system that keeps them imprisoned yet benefits all.

Very few things in life are black and white, right or wrong, good or bad; usually it's a mixture and that's how we get by and it works.

The Shift: How San Quentin Sparked My Transformation

I'm writing about San Quentin because, for me, it marked the beginning of a transformation I never thought was possible. It wasn't the prison walls or the routines that changed me—it was something deeper. Something internal. San Quentin became the mirror I needed to finally see myself clearly.

A Sea of Stories, Just Like Mine

What hit me first was how many men around me had stories that echoed my own—tales of broken homes, bad choices, and missed chances. We were all different, yet the same. That realization cracked something open in me.

For the first time, I didn't feel alone in my pain. I saw

my story reflected in the eyes of others—people who'd laughed, cried, and bled like I had. That connection, that shared struggle, planted the seed of empathy. It also woke me up to the reality that my life didn't have to end in regret. Change was possible. I saw it around me, in small ways—little miracles unfolding every day.

A Battle Inside My Mind

Everything did not get instantly better. That's too simple. I don't believe I deserved any special favor from God. But I do know this: when I started to shift my thinking—from bitterness and blame to ownership and growth—my life began to shift, too.

It started small. A better attitude. A single choice to react differently. A willingness to listen instead of arguing. Over time, those little decisions added up. Slowly, my outlook changed—and with it, my path.

This wasn't divine intervention. It was inner work. It was the result of facing my demons and deciding not to let them win. The real miracle wasn't external—it was the rewiring of my own mind.

The Power of a Thought

The biggest lesson I learned: your thoughts shape your reality. When I was stuck in negativity, everything around me seemed dark, but when I began to think in terms of growth, gratitude, and responsibility, opportunities appeared—people came into my life who helped, and I began helping others.

That shift didn't make life easy, but it made it meaningful. I learned to accept the past without letting it define me.

If You're in Your Own "San Quentin"

You might not be behind bars, but if you're stuck in a cycle of pain or regret, I want you to know this: You are not your worst decision. You are not beyond change.

Start small. Notice your thoughts. Challenge the ones that keep you stuck. Seek connection. Find someone who's been where you are and talk to them. And most of all—don't wait for a miracle. Be your own.

The first step isn't dramatic. It's quiet. It's the decision to believe that your story isn't over yet.

I left SQ with these new life experiences after 8 months.

SQ opened my eyes to look for something better something good something I could do for ever.

I next became a Deputy Sheriff at the Alameda County Sheriff Dept for 3 years.

I moved on to working on the Royal Viking Cruise Line 6 months.

I took 1 year off with-out working (my girlfriend supported me during this time).

The 1st of little miracles in my life happened.

I was using my girlfriends 1968 VW bug and loaded her car with the NY Sunday times and left my house at 5 am to deliver the papers. At 6 am I see as I am driving and tossing the big thick Sunday addition in a industrial park where I drive by about 6 people standing outside using air brushes painting four -7-foot monster suits at 6 am Sunday morning. I drove up to the group still in my car. A couple of the people outside looked over at me with a dead tired appearance. I said without getting out of the car,

"Wow, I wanted to do this" I said Those looking at me turned their heads back to the monster suits continuing to air brush without a word. The one closest to me painting monsters turned back to me and said, "Ok start at 8 am tomorrow" That s how it really happened and for the next 35 years I went from working in Special Effects shop to owning a Special Effects Shop called Creature FX

Inc. I traveled all over the world with this work and won a Tech. Academy Award for my Mechanical horse design and building. I am a voting member of the Academy, and I wrote this story for all those who are wondering, what am I going to do with my life?

To those who want to change their life.

Look for the best in yourself and you will find it.

A true story by
Mark Rappaport

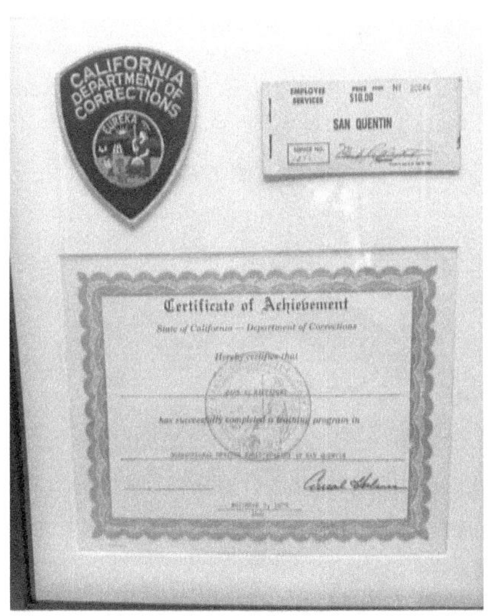

From Kevin Driscoll

The following is what Kevin Driscoll sent me in the mail on May 3, 2025. He is still incarcerated at the Honorable Donavan Rehabilitation Center in San Diego, California. While at San Quentin he played on the baseball team, mostly as a pitcher. He and I talk regularly on the telephone, 15-minute periods, several times a week, and have for years. He is able to do this through a program called Gettingout.com.

Mark Twain wrote: "It's not what you don't know that gets you in trouble. It's what you know that just isn't so that gets you into trouble."

This is one of my favorite quotes because unless we're masochists then it's the best life philosophy that we can have, especially if we are mindful, don't care to hurt anyone, and don't want to hurt ourselves.

Looking back on nearly three decades of incarceration, I realize the greatest pains and injuries I sustained were the ones that I earned through arrogance, not ignorance. The ignorance is a situation would cause me to pause. Awareness came gradually, in some cases about the ignorance of life, the system, and of what was happening right before my own eyes and ears. My own misperceptions and my erroneous judgments caused monumental suffering at times to myself and others. What's true is we do indeed cause most of if not all of our own suffering.

When we choose a rough road, a life of debauchery, the party lifestyle, and irresponsibility, why should it be surprising that there are so many bumps in the road that led to liquified intervals? And essentially give ourselves with our own consumption of the mental, emotional, spiritual, and psychological garbage we feed ourselves, our own indigestion. We don't need anyone to hate our guts, because we, by ourselves alone, hate our own guts.

An appropriate question is how do we consume more mindfully without generating unnecessary suffering or at least not adding to what we have accumulated? Really the answer we find is endeavoring to remain balanced. We can attempt to garner as much information as we can with an objective mindset, not having a bias or taking sides. By applying objectivity and thinking critically, we can observe consequential relationships. If we eat this spiritual fast food, then this is how it will look.

Our emotional or psychological regurgitation is a direct result of poor consumption, i.e., our greed, lust, laziness, etc. We took a shortcut, and we assumed we knew something we did not in fact know. Our own arrogance causes the deep suffering.

My deep suffering started because of my arrogance. I truly thought that I knew most if not all there was to know. I did not apply objective or critical thinking when I started. I was in a dreamlike fantasy of sorts and just wanted to get out of prison. On a deeper level I did not care who I hurt or what level of pain and suffering I caused. My primary concern was to satisfy myself with spiritual fast food, which is probably the best way to describe it. I caused myself and others around me great suffering.

My incarceration started December 4, 1998, but I had been in a prison of my own mind long before that. I was arrested on a Friday evening, right after a long work week. The time for my fiancées bridal shower came, but this was never to be.

I have been in jail or prison ever since. We had a terrible and violent argument, and she threatened the use of lethal force against me. We owned firearms, and during a physical fight, I grabbed one of the guns and shot her, killing her right then. What was worse was that her child from a former and broken marriage was present in the room. He endured incredible trauma, and as a result it haunts his life to this day. I have a great debt to pay for him and his family.

The only way over the years that I have been able to make personal amends is through service. To others around me. Living in prison in such a predatory environment, it is close to impossible, however. Most of us are broken of spirit and have little hope of anything better happening in our lives. Yet, through help of my family's support, I have furthered my education, earning a Jurist Doctorate degree in 2010 and became certified in American Sign Language (ASL). Also, I conduct a recovery group that teaches the Twelve Steps of Alcoholic/Narcotics Anonymous and as a result have seen numerous turnaround/success stories. We have even helped correctional officers and staff become sober with our example and positive efforts.

Along with our twelve-step recovery, Erik Menendez (yes, one of the brothers who was traumatically abused by his parents, which led to their death) developed a therapeutic group that uses meditation as a means to help heal the toxic shame that many of us experienced and which directly led us to prison.

The realization that many group participants have changed, moving from "we are bad," to that we committed actions that were "bad" helps lift the toxic shame from us, and the truly humane person who is inherently "good" emerges. This is not to say we are not criminally responsible for our actions but helps us understand the deeply complex dynamics present that set many of us on a collision course with the justice system. By acknowledging our past and our own emotional and psychological traumas, we can experience a degree of healing. Then rehabilitation and suitability for parole and release occurs.

Resisting and fighting became too much for us. We begin to cooperate, and the harshness of prison dissipates somewhat. Yet, in the environment we have found the ability to exist and become flexible. The biggest challenge in here is not the surly prison guard, not the 6'5" 285 lb. tough guy with an attitude. No! It's the person looking back at me in my acrylic mirror. I know as soon as I surrendered and became more accepting, God had a way of leading me. In recovery it's the Serenity Prayer. We accept things that can't be changed. We change the things that can be changed, and we have the wisdom to distinguish one from the other.

There is a famous saying that says, "It is what it is." I guess it is the same as John Lennon saying, "Let it be." Or was that Paul McCartney? We reach an age, and we know that out time is limited. We've done what we can do on the "inside" and it is time to go "outside." The debt, if it were possible, to quantify a human life could never be paid. Yet, through the suffering and pain we have experienced through the years, decades yes, we become on an elemental level instruments of stability and profound healing.

It's hard to describe the positivity that I feel every morning, even in the midst of what might seem to others' view as a clamatoes life — going to prison at age 25 for murdering my lover, nearly beaten to death by custody officers, twice nearly stabbed, once stabbed in the head, falsely set up as a drug dealer, having a snitch jacket put on me and treated with complete contempt by crooked correctional officers, among many other things. What keeps me going is that undying resolute hope and instinctively knowing that I will parole and that I'm heaven bound!

My father and mother never quit on me, and it took Covid-19 to stop them from visiting. I know in my head they are waiting for me. And inside or outside it doesn't matter in the end, because for everyone it truly is the relationship with God that matters.

We are not ex-convicts, ex-felons, inmates or whatever the world labels us as. Although we are "justice impacted" people, we are people. Many of us have learned life lessons on the "inside" and we have much love to bring "outside." Don't be afraid of us! Welcome us because people outside will soon find there are many better people inside than out.

Kevin at bat:

Following are Kevin's thoughts on "Suboxone":

Good morning, Kent! You asked if I would write a little about the suboxone program. What would be a good response? The short of it? It's terrible. Yet, we realize there's so much more to it. Why? We are dealing with serious addiction. The addiction process can manifest in so many ways. Substance abuse is just the lowest rung on the ladder. One of the results of childhood trauma.

Addiction. We self sooth through the ability to control our environment, our feelings, our beliefs, and our thoughts. Essentially the human being is his/her thoughts, emotions, and sense perceptions. Most in prison or in society at large are not afforded an adequate education to think objectively/critically. Most.

Are we incapable of independent thought? Sadly, this includes many of the staff. It's not their fault. The education system in this country has failed them. Who gravitates to work at a prison? Very few, and the environment totally corrupts. It is dog-eat-dog for lack of a better term. Suboxone is a method of control.

Drugs help only the ones who market and sell it. This control has men lining up to get their fix, but it doesn't get people better. It seems people want to avoid pain, but pain is the only way to healing. It's sad to watch this Suboxone distribution. The men take the patch that's meant to dissolve in the mouth and inject it. This subjects them to all the bacteria in their mouths.

It's extremely dangerous, but who cares when 300 or more of my neighbors are condemned to death by the State of California. Sterilize the lethal injection needle? Get real!

The program is psychological control. All brought to you by CCPOA, the modern-day Nazi party. Very sad to say the least.

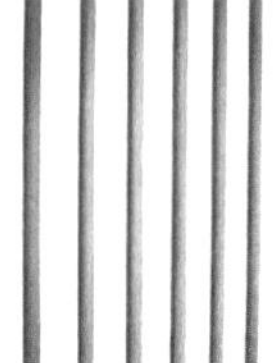

From Dean Taylor

After more than three decades in law enforcement, I believed I had a thorough understanding of our justice system—its strengths, its flaws, and its guiding principles. But nothing prepared me for what it felt like to be on the receiving end of it.

Not long ago, I experienced a disturbing situation at my home. A group of teenagers repeatedly banged on my front door, for two consecutive weekends late in the evening. Concerned for my safety and property, I did what any responsible citizen would do, after the tenth time: I called the police. No one arrived.

After waiting, I stepped outside, confronted the group, and caught one of the boys. I calmly offered him a choice: I could call the police again, have them show up, and have him arrested, or I could drive him home. He chose the ride home. When we arrived at his house we rang the doorbell, no one was there. It wasn't until an hour later that I learned his parents were dining at a restaurant just a block from my home.

That's when the police finally arrived—not to assist me, but to arrest me.

Despite my full cooperation, I was not read my Miranda

rights. I was taken into custody, processed, and charged with four felonies. What followed was a four-year ordeal that tested not just my patience, but my faith in the system I once served.

Eventually, the charges were dropped. The court granted me diversion which eventually led to the charges being dropped. I am grateful for that outcome, and I respect the process that allowed this to happen, but along the way several violations of my constitutional rights occurred, violations no citizen should ever have to experience.

Due process and the presumption of innocence must not depend on perception or position. I was treated as guilty from the moment of contact, and my legal protections—against self-incrimination, for due process, and for immediate legal counsel—were disregarded. During this whole process no member of the arresting agency or the District Attorney's Office ever asked me what happened, despite having video of all ten incidence of them banging on my door.

I share this not out of bitterness, but with purpose. My story is not unique. Many Americans find themselves trapped in a system that often presumes guilt first and asks questions later, and in my case no questions were ever asked. As my African American partner of eight years said to me the day after my arrest, welcome to the world of a young black man in America. If it can happen to a retired officer, it can happen to anyone.

Justice is not merely the end result—it's the process. It must be fair, timely, and rooted in the Constitution. We owe that to every citizen, regardless of their background, their status, or their past service.

It's time to reflect, reform, and recommit to the principles that define our justice system—not only when it's easy, but when it's hardest to uphold.

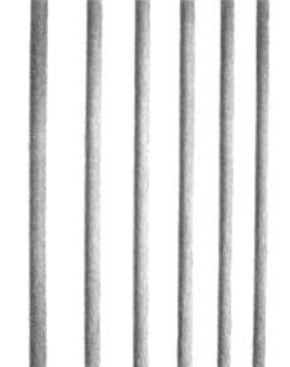

From George*

The Shift: How San Quentin Sparked My Transformation

I'm writing about San Quentin because, for me, it marked the beginning of a transformation I never thought was possible. It wasn't the prison walls or the routines that changed me— it was something deeper. Something internal. San Quentin became the mirror I needed to finally see myself clearly.

A Sea of Stories, Just Like Mine

What hit me first was how many men around me had stories that echoed my own—tales of broken homes, bad choices, and missed chances. We were all different, yet the same. That realization cracked something open in me.

For the first time, I didn't feel alone in my pain. I saw my story reflected in the eyes of others—people who'd laughed, cried, and bled like I had. That connection, that shared struggle, planted the seed of empathy. It also woke me up to the reality that my life didn't have to end in regret. Change was possible. I saw it around me, in small ways— little miracles unfolding every day.

A Battle Inside My Mind

I won't lie and say I found God and everything instantl got

better. That's too simple. I don't believe I deserved any-special favor from God. But I do know this: when I started to shift my thinking—from bitterness and blame to owner-ship and growth—my life began to shift, too.

It started small. A better attitude. A single choice to react differently. A willingness to listen instead of arguing. Over time, those little decisions added up. Slowly, my out-look changed—and with it, my path.

This wasn't divine intervention. It was inner work. It was the result of facing my demons and deciding not to let them win. The real miracle wasn't external—it was the rewiring of my own mind.

The Power of a Thought

The biggest lesson I learned. Your thoughts shape your reality. When I was stuck in negativity, everything around me seemed dark. But when I began to think in terms of growth, gratitude, and responsibility, opportunities appeared—people came into my life who helped, and I began helping others.

That shift didn't make life easy, but it made it meaning-ful. I learned to accept the past without letting it define me.

If You're in Your Own "San Quentin"

You might not be behind bars, but if you're stuck in a cycle of pain or regret, I want you to know this: You are not your worst decision. You are not beyond change.

Start small. Notice your thoughts. Challenge the ones that keep you stuck. Seek connection. Find someone who's been where you are and talk to them. And most of all—don't wait for a miracle. Be your own.

The first step isn't dramatic. It's quiet. It's the decision to believe that your story isn't over yet.

(*not his real name)

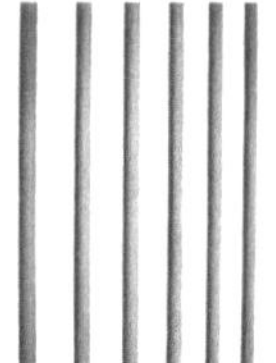

From Curtis Roberts

Freedom after 29 Years

It was a brisk December day when the prison van drove me from the inmate population to the front gate of San Quentin State Prison, the year was 2018.

I was scared, free but scared. And what I now know is that the day I walked into freedom was great and all, but I did not have a clue to what freedom really was. My mind still acted and reacted as if I was still a inmate. My path to being free was much like that of peeling an onion a layer at a time. Let me give you a example of a situation that really happened to me. Driving for the first time in three decades was amazing, it wasn't like anything I have experienced before and it was after about three months of driving that I said to my wife "...look at that new billboard." My wife gently said to me, sweetie that billboard has been up for years now. It was at that moment in time that all a long I had been driving in tunnel vision. And living my daily life the same way. Here I am seven years later looking back at those early days of my release. Such tender moments they were, even childlike.

My days now are filled with work which I love to do, well

work is really ministry yeah working for God. Love it. Love it. I heard it said that it's a gift to go to bed exhausted doing the Lord's work.

Pastor Kent started teaching me and mentoring me some 30 years ago, I guess you can say I learned well. Today my life is filled with helping the homeless, giving food and clothing, spending time with them. And I also get to go back inside prisons, so far San Quentin, Jacksonville prison, and Logan prison. I can honestly tell you it brought great joy to me walking back inside San Quentin prison which I have done twice knowing that SQ didn't beat me. Today, I am married, a homeowner, and living with such joy and wonder as each day unfolds. It's like my Heavenly Father has released me into this big ole' playground that we call the world and asks me to just go out and be who I made you to be. Portia Nelson wrote, *I walk down the street. There is a deep hole, I fall in. I am lost...I am helpless. it's not my fault and takes forever to get out.*

Next time I walk down the street there is a deep hole, and I pretend that I don't see it. I fall in again. I can't believe I am in this same place. But it isn't my fault. It takes a long time to get out.

I walk down the same street, there is a deep hole, I see it, I fall in, but this time I know where I am and get out immediately.

I walk down the same street, there is a deep hole, I walk around it.

Lastly, I walk down a different street.

Today I walk down the street with a hole (prison) I see it and instead of walking down a different street I jump into the hole and show the prisoners how to get out.

The End
Curtis Roberts, 2026

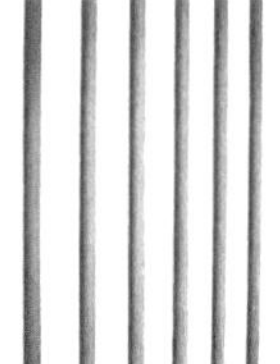

Dealing with Our Guilt

Just yesterday, March 29, 2026, while sitting on benches that line the front porch of our Miller Avenue Church in Mill Valley, waiting for the morning service to begin, a discussion arose about facing guilt from our wrongdoings. Just three of us there, and we all admitted that we had to face this, and one of us was being plagued by it, and fairly severely, right then.

At one point in the conversation, I talked about how some who had been or were still in prison, had talked to me about this very thing. They talked about awful feelings of guilt would rise up within them, that would not let go of them. And I will admit I have had to, and still am to this day, am haunted by a powerful sense of grief, guilt, remorse, and more. Yes, I admit it, in fact these sensations/feelings have actually grown more powerful as the years pass.

You are reading this from a long-time pastor who knows he has been forgiven of his sinful acts, even ones I would not ever mention to anyone.

Yes, I know my awful deeds are washed away through the power of my Savior. Yet, these remain in my heart and mind, and they seem to cause more unpleasantness as time goes on. Wish I could offer encouraging words, but I do not find them. I bring this up so that others who are like suffering will not feel they are alone, or that there are unforgiven awful folk.

A last word: during the 1970s I did counselling work along with being a pastor, and I did this four days a week at the Marin Christian Counselling Center on Fourth Street in San Rafael, next door to a McDonalds's restaurant. Never charged a penny, and I heard some terribly depressing stories, some from pastors of churches, who confessed to awful deeds. Funny, I recall these just now and I decided to include a word on this.

I have no satisfying explanation to offer, all I can do is say that if such happens to others, you, know that it is not uncommon, and it is best to talk with others about it. Find a friend, go to a counsellor, a psychologist, a therapist, a pastor, and get it out. And, above all, bring your concerns to the One who knows and loves you.

-Kent

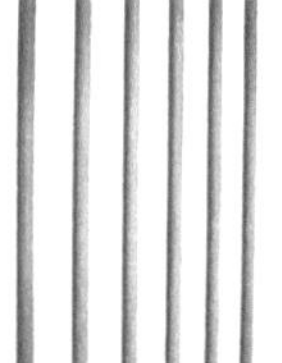

Baseball at the Lower Yard of SQ Prison

2009 Baseball Season Reflections

Field Conditions and Challenges

Some of the coldest and windiest days I have experienced were spent on the ball field at San Quentin's lower yard. The outfield was bumpy and scarred, with goose droppings scattered by aggressive birds that could not be disturbed, as the prison administration had adopted environmentally friendly policies. The infield consisted of dirt with numerous rocks and narrow canyons carved by rain, stretching for yards. Unfortunately, the tools needed to fix these hazards were considered "weapons stock" and were not allowed in inmates' hands. While metal and wood bats were permitted, these did not qualify as tools.

A strong wind usually blew out of right field directly into our faces as we sat in the third base dugout. The wind would force infield dirt into clothing, hair, eyes, ears, and mouth, turning a black shirt brown and serving as proof of the harsh conditions. The prison maintenance staff struggled with the irrigation system, resulting in pools of water around shortstop and second base, with right field being especially soggy and treacherous. A broken sprinkler head seemed to have gone unresolved for years, making right field a minefield for players.

Tryouts and Team Formation

Tryouts began in late February, with two days held on consecutive Saturday mornings. Although the players were not desperate to make the teams, they were disappointed when told they did not make it. After the first day, about half a dozen hopefuls were informed face-to-face that they had no chance, often because they could not catch or throw the ball. Despite claims of having played professional or major league baseball, these abilities—or lack thereof—were easily revealed during simple catching drills. The opportunity to play baseball in prison was meaningful and fun, and even though some players exaggerated their talents, most coaches could quickly assess skill levels.

Two teams of fifteen players each were selected from over fifty who tried out: the "A" team Giants and the "B" team Pirates. The Giants got first pick, while the Pirates took the remaining players. Initially, there was a clear difference in skill levels, but as the season progressed, the gap began to close.

The Origins of Baseball at San Quentin

The modern era of baseball at San Quentin Prison began in 1995 with Earl Smith, the Protestant Chaplain, who later became chaplain for the San Francisco Giants and the San Francisco 49ers. In 2000, the Giants' equipment manager, Mike Murphy, provided uniforms for San Quentin's Pirates, turning them into the Giants. Dan Jones and I had coached the Pirates, and with Chaplain Smith's encouragement in 1997, the team transitioned from Pirates to

Giants. Some players preferred the Giants name, questioning the appropriateness of Pirates for a prison team. However, team captain Jason Gottlieb, a devoted Pirate, initially walked off in protest but ultimately decided to stay with the team.

Scheduling and Administrative Support

Before the first game on April 4, nearly eighty games were scheduled—forty for each team. I handled scheduling, while Elliot Smith managed gate clearances for visiting teams from the Bay Area Senior Men's League, a task I had managed for thirteen years and disliked for its demands. Laura Bowman and her team efficiently managed player clearances. The San Quentin administration, including the warden's office and correctional officers, worked diligently to keep the baseball program running. Coaches contributed what resources they could, as there was no state budget for the teams, and all were unpaid volunteers.

The Giants played on Wednesday evenings and Saturday mornings, while the Pirates played Thursday and Saturday evenings. Game schedules were subject to change, especially due to disruptions like the arrival of the swine flu, which led to a two-week shutdown.

Coaching Staff and Season Records

The Giants were coached by Kevin Loughlin, Mike Deeble, and Elliot Smith. I coached the Pirates alongside Stan Damas and Len Zemarkowitz. Len took over during my one-month vacation, but due to lockdowns, the Pirates played only two games, losing both. For the season, the Pirates played twenty-one games, with a record of 7 wins and 13 losses, hoping to reach 8 wins. Last year, with only one team, the Giants, the record was 35 wins and 10 losses. Having two teams thinned the talent but provided more opportunities for players, which was valued by both coaches and prison administration.

Preparing for the Big Game

Kevin Loughlin, the Giants' head coach, was scheduled to be away on business and asked me to manage the Giants for the game against Benicia on Saturday morning, August 15. This meant a double-header for me, just returning from vacation. Benicia cancelled the day before, prompting a decision not to invite them back in 2010, and The Willing, my own team, faced similar issues with fielding enough players.

The Willing had been special to me, originating from a connection with Shane Kennedy during my daughters' Little League years. Shane, a seasoned coach and player, brought a team of local coaches, The Willing, into the prison for thirteen years, becoming a favorite opponent. Many friendships formed through these games, but as with all baseball careers, those days eventually ended, leaving coaching as a way to stay connected to the game.

To fill the Giants' roster for Saturday morning, I sent a plea to seven faithful teams, and four responded—Sting, All Blacks, Barons, and The Mission—providing ten players and ensuring the game would go on, thanks to the internet and email.

Game Day Management and Team Dynamics

At the Thursday game, August 13, Pirates vs. The Fog, I informed Giants catcher Johnny Taylor that I would be managing the Saturday game. Kevin and I had coached together previously, and I now served as general manager over baseball, softball, and football programs. Having an outside coach in charge was standard practice to avoid issues, and I hoped to prepare the Giants for the upcoming game, despite some players seeing me as "the enemy" due to team rivalry.

On Saturday morning, some Giants starters were unhappy about being benched initially, but my plan was to play everyone and rotate starters in halfway. This was justified due to limited games caused by swine flu. All Giants players got at least two at-bats and played half the game. The Giants won decisively with 17 hits, and Chris "Stretch" Rich pitched a complete game. Despite the victory, there was less camaraderie than usual, with some players ignoring me. However, the core group appreciated the opportunity to play and adapted to changes.

Final Showdown: Giants vs. Pirates

This was the third and final meeting of the season between the Giants and Pirates, with tensions running high. The game started late due to new policies, and players hesitated to dress in uniforms, which had become dirty and smelly due to lack of washing facilities. With encouragement, both teams dressed out, though the field was not stripped, giving the game a makeshift feel and adding to the tension.

Israel Amos, who had previously refused to play for me, set aside differences to join the Pirates for this game, his only appearance of the season. With a 14-man roster, I aimed to play each man half the game, balancing the desire to win with the importance of participation. David Baker started as pitcher, while Herman Hopkins, the other starter, had played Thursday. The Pirates took an early lead, but the Giants tied and then went ahead. The Pirates tied again in the fifth.

Two suicide squeeze plays were attempted, neither

successful, but they kept the Giants alert to unconventional strategies.

Games usually ended around 7:50 PM due to the need for Close B inmates to appear for a count at North Block, with players from both teams required to participate. Time was a factor, but with the game tied, stopping was undesirable.

Sixth Inning: Decisive Moments

David Baker pitched in the top of the sixth, getting the first batter out, then allowing a hit and a walk, followed by a strikeout. With two outs and time running out, Red Casey, known for clutch home runs, was intentionally walked, loading the bases. I signaled to pitch to Deuce, the Giants' hottest hitter. The first pitch was high and inside, leading to a weak grounder to first for an easy out, ending the inning. The Pirates now had a chance to win.

Bottom of the Sixth: Pirates' Victory

Israel led off, and despite looking awkward on two swings, worked a full count and hit a double into the left field corner. Kevin Henry, a strong and well-liked player, was up next. On the first pitch, a curveball, Israel advanced to third on a passed ball. The Giants brought the infield in, and Mario Ellis, under pressure, pitched high and outside. Henry reached out and hit the ball toward right field. Israel tagged up and waited, but the ball kept drifting and went over the fence for a home run—or possibly a double, depending on perspective. Regardless, it secured the win for the Pirates.

Aftermath and Reflections

The Pirates celebrated as if it were the final game of the World Series, gathering around Henry as he crossed home plate. David Baker called the team to the mound, delivered a brief statement about trusting in Jesus, closed with a prayer, and rallied the team before everyone packed up and returned to their respective units. It was 8 PM.

Frankie Smith, the Giants' inmate coach, approached me afterward, shook hands, and congratulated me on a good game—a fine gesture. The game became a cherished memory for all involved, providing a pleasant moment in a cold and windy place.

Kent Philpott
August 28, 2009

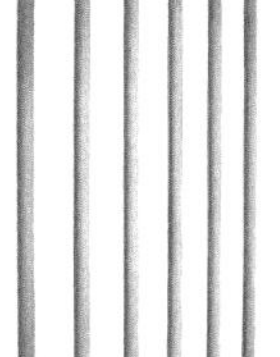

Highlights of the 2010 Baseball Season at SQ

How the season begins

Tryouts were Feb 27 and March 6—on the lower yard, but on the asphalt, which there is not much of, due to the new hospital.

I am Kent Philpott, age 68, pastor over 4 decades, now in my 26th year at Miller Avenue Baptist Church in Mill Valley, California. Converted while in the military at age 21, I am so very pleased to be a follower of Jesus Christ. Fifteen years ago, I began managing baseball teams at San Quentin, this after fourteen years doing ministry out of the Garden Protestant Chapel. When asked what I do, I say I am a teacher of the Bible to believers and a preacher of the Gospel to unbelievers. As a coach at the prison my pulpit is along the third base line—the 3rd base coaches box. My work is to glorify God.

Prior to the tryouts, Kevin Loughlin, Len Zemarkowitz, and I met together (Elliot Smith, Stan Damas, and Mike Deeble could not make it), at Pinky's Pizza in San Rafael to discuss how we would handle the upcoming season. In the past, I have always argued for a larger number of players, while most others thought a smaller number on the team would be easier on everyone—but maybe a smaller number like 17 would work. My suggestion was that we wait and see how many players came out and go by that. One thing we were all sure of—certain players would not be on the team. Some of them we considered to be "poison," and a few others we thought were simply not good enough to remain on the team, though they were veterans. Of course, our decisions were not going to be greeted with smiles, but it would have to done for the sake of the team as well as the peace of mind of the coaches.

First day of tryouts

Feb 27 turned out to be a cold and rainy day, but we went on with the tryouts anyway. About forty men came out. We began by playing catch—pairing the players up. The coaches walked around with clip boards noting the ones who at least could throw and catch. What caught my eye was that there were a whole flock of new young guys, mostly black, and some looked like ball players. There were a few guys I cut on that first day—anyone would be able to see that baseball was not their game. There were five of these, older convicts, who wanted to be a part of the most elite group in the prison, a team that had received national attention more than a few times. Making cuts is the most unpleasant part of the process, for me, and as head coach it is up to me to do it. It is not enough to post a list of the people who are on the team. Some guys, I had learned over the years, took it way too hard when they couldn't find their names on the roster. Maybe I shouldn't care about that and save myself some sleep, but I have not yet gotten that hard inside.

The trick is not to become hard inside, which happens to many of the correctional officers and other staffers at any prison. It has been said that I am hard on the outside but soft on the inside. An overly simple assessment, I think; I like to think I am more complex than that. Surely I am soft on the outside or the people I am pastor of would not tolerate me. And if I were really hard on the inside, then I would think I am not enough aware of grace and mercy. Jesus did save me from my sins, which were many, so I know what it is, to some degree, what it is to be loved and forgiven. This I have to give to those guys who have been rejected and neglected and made to feel themselves unlovable. Hard inside? I have to be, I suppose, but I am hoping my little light shines through anyway.

Second day of tryouts

March 6's weather was better, and we were able to use parts of the field where the rain had not created little lakes. Even more convicts were out now—the word having gotten around. Posters had been placed, thanks to our supervisor Don DeNevi, in North Block and in H Unit. (Within these two "housing" units, North Block being the traditional cell block and H Unit the dorm style, were about 1,800 men.)

The count was about forty-five, and some old guys (not as old as me, but guys way past their prime by a decade or so) were there also. One guy put his name down as Vito Genovese and said yes when asked if he was part of that family. We didn't believe it.

The field conditions were so good we did not feel we needed to extend tryouts one more week. Our coaches really worked it—throwing, fielding, hitting, base running—a good chance to see everyone. We would not want it said that that we did not get a good look at everyone.

After nearly three hours of baseball, the coaches retreated to the dugout on the third base side, the Giants' dugout, and sat down with our clip boards. The list of guys we thought should make the team was longer than we hoped for in the beginning—twenty-two. Besides that, we knew there would be more convicts showing up for weeks—new arrivals or others who talked themselves into giving it a try.

There were thoughts of shortening the list, but I argued for the full number. I reminded the other coaches that the previous year, 2009, we had two teams, the Giants and the Pirates, and at the end of the year the Giants had thirteen players and the Pirates eleven—I meant that there has always been an attrition rate in operation, at least that I had observed this over the last fourteen years that I had been there. This was persuasive, so we carried the lot.

Let me spend a moment more on the attrition rate. Baseball, for one thing, is not an easy game to play. Over the years I have noticed that athletes engaged in other sports and excelled in them could not play baseball well. Baseball is a game of unusual skills that must be in combination. Speed, hand-eye coordination, body strength from head to toe, agility, stamina (it is a very long season), and more than anything else, the emotional strength to deal with failure. Baseball, it is often said, is a humbling game. You will be humbled when there you are alone on the field having screwed up. Right in front of your world you drop the ball, strike out with the bases loaded in the last inning, throw the ball away and runners are circling the bases— and for guys who had known little more than continual failure, it could be difficult. Courage may be the single most important element for a baseball player—baseball, it is said, is 90% mental, 10% athletic ability. And in San Quentin there are other factors at play.

When a person goes to prison it may be years before he (there is no she at SQ) accepts the fact he is there. It is so hard to come to terms with freedom, family, community, job, love, fun—all being lost, at least for a while, sometimes a very long while. Now a life is shot, the future gone, at minimum marred horribly for all time, and all you have is the ubiquitous ugliness that is prison. Not only is San Quentin ugly and dirty beyond description, but the real awfulness is being with whom you must be with, and there is no way to be alone and apart from the twistedness of life that winds up in our prisons. Therefore, convicts will develop a life of delusion. Guys have told me they can throw a fast ball a 100 miles per hour, or that they played major league baseball, and so on. Delusion, illusion, and confusion—all to find a way to live in ugliness and despair. When the realities of baseball life descend upon the deluded and they are shown up for what they are, some will quit.

Of course, there are the injuries, and we have more than our share, because there is little chance for true conditioning. Then, some will do something stupid and get thrown in the hole—that is, segregation or solitary—for one reason or another. It is not unusual to find that a player has been transferred to another prison, or, and this is the best reason, they were released and are now at home, if they had a home.

Making the cuts

With the tryouts concluded, everyone was then called out to the mound. Important meetings are always held at the pitcher's mound. The other convicts are then too far away to hear what is going on, and it is almost a sacred place, this place where the pitcher delivers the ball.

The moment I dreaded had arrived. I knew it would be a major disappointment to a number of the veterans, guys that had almost become friends.

I read the names of the players who had made the team. Very silent and tense was the way I would describe the event. Two of the older guys, both of whom were on the "poison" list, stood away from the group with their arms folded across their chests staring at the ground. They knew what was likely to happen—their names would not be called. Word would get around quickly, like it always does at the prison because the prison is a rumor mill. Bad news travels fast.

After the team was announced, I invited people who did not make the team to come talk with me. As the crowd dispersed, I saw several of those who had been cut and had played for me for years, and I saw they were upset. For awhile, they could not speak with me but got together with other coaches and talked with them. After some time, maybe ten minutes, one by one these guys drifted over to me, and one by one I listened to what they had to say.

On the one hand I felt sorry for them. The coveted privilege to play baseball while in prison had been lost, and it was a genuine loss, perhaps not like losing a friend or parent to death, but a loss, nevertheless. They would not be dressed out in San Francisco Giants uniforms on April 17, opening day, when the warden threw out the first pitch, when there was a color guard and the national anthem sung. They would not be interviewed by members of the media, or line up along the third base line and introduced as the 2010 San Quentin Giants Club. They would not be in the team photo or the individual photo shoots I always took, and which would also be posted on www.flickr.com for their families to see. These cut players would now be a part of the blue, sad mass of convicts who gathered on the lower yard every evening to do nothing.

Loss of youth

But then again, I knew it had to be done. I remember the sensation, the flood of emotions that came over me when

I knew my reflexes were no longer good enough to get me out of the way of a line drive. In fact, I can no longer stand at third base and make the calls because of this; I am forced to making the calls from the bench.

One of the easiest paths to deal with loss is the one they took—anger, anger at me. Some of these guys had known me for a decade and a half. For some few maybe, I had become a father figure, a sub-father most of them had never had. Doubtless no one would try to harm me, but it was a possibility, and I had already been warned that there could be retaliation if one particular guy did not make the team…he had not.

One by one I listened to the complaints and the pleas and did my best to make the reason for the cuts as humane as I could. I quoted the great prophet, and yes I thought some imagined I would mention Isaiah, Jeremiah, or even Mohammed as there are a couple Muslims on the team, but no, I quoted Clint Eastwood, from the first Dirty Harry movie, "a man must know his limitations." It didn't help; the guys were just going to be mad.

For many of these men, their reality was having a reservoir of anger fueled by either booze or dope or a combination thereof that had led some of the men to prison. Anger management is a course/class most inmates have taken. In fact, if there isn't at least one anger management class listed in a prisoner's file, the parole board is not impressed.

Eight guys who were counting on making the team did not. In a certain sense it signaled the end of their youth, even for those who were fifty-plus years old. As long as you can play baseball, you are not old—this may be what some think, and in prison a convict is frozen solid with the fear that his life is slipping away little by little. It is the worst nightmare.

The fall out, or pay back

March 6 was a Saturday, and Monday morning early I got a call from the prison. My boss wanted me to come in for a meeting. I did and explained myself. The people who supervise the recreation program supported me. But it was not over, since a group of the cut veterans demanded there be a second team like there had been in 2009. Another meeting was called, and I had to go in. But Don, the state employee who had really put the recreation program at the prison on the map, told me of the issues the convicts would bring up, thus giving me a chance to prepare myself.

The last thing I wanted was a second team. The trash talk, the ugly, mean attitudes—I had been through it before, and I would not and could not deal with it again. As best I could, I challenged and denied every point. At the same time, I gave in to some. There could be a second team but supervised by one of my coaches, and the team would not play outside teams, would not be the Pirates and have the old uniforms, and they could have every other Monday evening and every other Saturday evening to practice and play inter-mural games. There was one big No! This team would never play the Giants.

The bottom line with me was to keep the program up and running. It would not take much to close it down. One fight on the field, or in North Block, or in H Unit—that would be it. If I gave in, I would be taken advantage of and most importantly, lose the respect of the convicts. The same goes for any convict. If one is found to be weak, he will be taken advantage of, and it could be of a sexual nature. Sex is always just under the surface. Occasionally, we hear of a someone being taken out of the prison in hand cuffs—correctional officers, volunteers, state employees—and the reasons could be a long list, but it often involves bringing in drugs, cell phones, and cigarettes, with sexual contact also high on the list.

Power and authority

The meeting went well, and all sides agreed to the deal. There was no choice, really, because I was not going to go along with the agenda the rebel team wanted.

One of the troubles with being a coach is you have a certain amount of power, and that power can be easily abused. Studies have shown it is the human tendency to abuse others under our authority. Circumstances will arise where decisions have to be made and authority must be exercised. And the best of us can fall right into the trap. Over a fifty-year span I have coached many baseball teams, of many different descriptions, and I have abused my authority on occasion. Additionally, I have seen many coaches abuse players verbally and physically. This is nothing new, but I hate to find it in myself. I am a pastor of a Baptist Church with some forty-two years of ministry behind me, and I am fully aware of how quickly spiritual authority can be abused—and I am guilty here.

How many of us grew up being abused? It is safe to say that being abused, bullied, and treated badly by people in authority over us, like parents, teachers, coaches, cops, and so on, will impact us. How many convicts were abused while kids? Abuse creates all kinds of negativity like not caring, being angry and vengeful, and needing to escape a horrible reality with a little help from pharma. If I abuse the authority I have, what separates me from the problem?

2010 Giants set

The team was set—maybe. In the course of one week seven new inmates wanted to try out. For many years my procedure has been the same—play catch with the prospect. I say, "Take this glove, I've got mine, let's go out to left field and play catch. And you will have to be a phenom to make the team." Now, a phenom, as in phenomenal, is a person who is so good we absolutely must have him on the team. To be a phenom you must either be one heck of a pitcher or short stop or center fielder or catcher.

Up the middle—these are the positions that demand the highest priority. And they must be able to hit, since these position players are usually the best athletes. But—this is not always true.

Now I have a convict with me in left field, and he is scared, anxious, tense, and wants to impress me. First off, I tell him to throw easy. I tell him I will know if he can play simply by watching the way he throws, not how fast he throws. Despite my instruction, many a man has done his arm some damage in that single try out. Rotator cuffs torn, even bicep muscles torn. Sadly, the would-be player turns away in discouragement. It is form, balance, and proper technique that matters to a coach. Some get it, and then I lead them to the dugout and grab a bat. "Show me your swing and show me how you bunt."

Usually, for a convict who has been down for a long time, I am going to see a softball swing, an upper cut, and for the right hander the right wrist shifts low with the left wrist on top for a smooth lift swing. Great for a softball player; disaster for a baseball player. I am hoping to see a short, compact, level swing through the zone with the head in. One guy had it—a big, tough-looking, white guy, tattooed like a gang banger. Then he told me he could pitch, so we went back to the bull pen, and he did have good balance and an easy motion. His stretch was solid, he kept the ball low, so he was a phenom. Later on in the practice he hit a ton and played a smooth first base. Now a confession: he had no cleats, only prison issue slippers. The very next practice I brought him a size 13 shoe from the San Francisco Giants. Don't tell anyone.

Twenty-two players made the team. Inside of two weeks, the team was reduced to eighteen players. One went to the hole, solitary, for trying to sell pictures hanging on the chapel wall to volunteers. Then another one was caught stealing other convicts' personal property out of their lockers in H Unit. Another twisted his ankle badly playing basketball, and then one fellow, who could probably see he would not get much playing time, simply stopped showing up at practices. From twenty-two to eighteen.

3% cut

One of my jobs is to set the schedule. This year there is a possibility we will play as many as 60 games. Within two weeks the game dates were taken. Thank God for the internet and email. The way it was broken down was the Giants would play Wednesday and Thursday nights and Saturday mornings. Fine, I was ahead of the game.

Then it was announced, via email, that due to a mandatory cut in the California State budget, all program costs had to be reduced by 3%. It impacted the teams because the Wednesday games were taken away because of staffing shortages that would be imposed—there would be no lower yard officers available on Wednesdays. But then I received word, via email, that there was a change. Thursday would be taken and Wednesday given back.

At some point the baseball managers of the outside teams will begin to think I am crazy. Maybe they would be right. I worry about whether the visiting outside team will be cleared in or not. One time, and this was the worst, a team came up from Los Angeles, came up the day before the game, a Friday, stayed overnight, showed up at the

East Gate promptly at 8:30 a.m. Saturday morning, only to find that there had been a racially motivated fight on the lower yard and that the prison was completely locked down—nothing would happen. The disappointment they felt was unleashed on me in the parking lot. They did not realize the chanciness in coming to a prison expecting a baseball game.

I was asked to do this San Quetin baseball coaching by the chaplain many years ago. I said yes, and I want to stick by my word, not that I stick by all my words, but everyone knows I am a Christian, and I want to have a good testimony. Two, I love baseball, and this allows me to stay around the game. Three, after years of doing cell to cell witnessing and giving out Christian literature, I found that being with the men on the yard directly, and that over the course of many months, my opportunity to talk about Jesus increased. Four, then due to the media attention the team attracts, the somewhat feeble witness I have has been multiplied many times.

For the record

Before I quit here, a few more comments—for the record. The prison has no way to get our uniforms washed. The laundry is sent to Solano Prison. My guys tell me it is a disaster, so that most of them have been washing their own clothes—in their cells. Then there are no lawn mowers to cut the Field of Dreams grass. Yes, Field of Dreams. About 2001 the wonderful San Francisco Giants created our playing field lawn, even sending in their experts to do it for us. (We do thank our beloved chaplain Earl Smith, now retired.) There is no way to cut the grass, though. At the conclusion of the last meeting to meet the expectations of the cut players, I was informed that we needed two lawn mowers to cut the grass. I raised my hand. One day later, my wife, Katie, whom many of the convicts know because she has both preached and sung at the chapel and most recently has sat beside me and kept score, refurbished an extra power model we had. And it works with one pull. This will be her ticket into the opening day seat right next to me in the San Quentin Giants' dugout—if the warden approves.

EPILOGUE FROM TWO YEARS LATER:

Below is a copy of the email I sent out to the managers of the teams so far scheduled to come into the prison in 2012. It was my duty to let them know this. There were virtually no coaches left to run two teams, two practices a week, and two games against outside teams per week. There was no other choice.

Hello Everyone,

A sad time for me and for you and your players: there will be no season at the prison this year. I am hoping that, after the dust settles, that we will have a 2013 season. Let me tell you in a greatly abbreviated form, however, what brought us to this point.

One, considerable trouble among our coaches. (How's that for brief?)

Two, utterly unsafe conditions. Some months ago, West Block went gen¬eral population, that is, mainline prisoners, 800 plus of them, occupied the block. Due to budget concerns, these Level 3 convicts, by the stroke of an administra¬tion pen, became Level 2. This meant they were all eligible to come down on the 108 yard and par-ticipate in the sports programs. My first sight of them was when I went with my son Vernon, who runs the flag football program, to observe two games. One look and I could see that everything had changed. Young, aggressive, three race groups, white (looked like the Hell's Angel's rejects due to being too rowdy), blacks, and Hispanics, all ganged up and looking to figure out who was going to call the shots, deal the dope, and control some rather unsavory realities of prison life.

I cannot, after what has happened in the last few days, justify inviting anyone into the prison right now. There will be those who will disagree with me, but I have to act according to my conscience. I have done the inviting and the scheduling, so the burden is on me. I am aware that there would be those who would push for the season to move along anyway, but it is my view that this is not only impossible but dangerous. The final decision was made clear to me this morning when I got a letter of resignation from the coach I have been working with for years. We actually have coached the Giants together for the last two years, and he cited safety concerns.

So, there we are. Perhaps there will be a 2013 season, but things have to shake out so we can see what kind of adjustments are made. Word I have is that it takes a year or so before the hierarchy is established and the pecking order made plain.

Thank you for being willing to come in and play our guys.

Kent Philpott Books

Serving in Marin: Stories from the Life of a Process Server (2025)

Fundamentos Cristianos: Lecciones, debates y conversasiones (2025)

Ball Four, Take Your Base!: Baseball at San Quentin, the 2011 & 2012 Seasons (2025)

Who Are the Curanderos? ¿Quienes son los Curanderos? (Little Book) (2024)

Coming to My Last Days (on the Planet) (2024)

Why I Decided Not to Kill Myself (2023)

Pathways to Darkness: Exposing the Dangers of Contemporary Spiritualities (2023)

For Those Who Have Made Shipwreck of Their Faith (2023)

A Manual of Demonology and the Occult (2023)

Who Is Muhammad's Gabriel? (2022)

Strike Three, You're Out! Baseball at San Quentin; the 2010 Season (2021)

Líbranos del Mal: Cómo Jesús Echa Fuera Demonios Hoy (Spanish Edition, 2021)

Deliverance Handbook: A Guide to Casting Out Demons for Today's Christian (2021)

A Marriage Manual for Former Homosexuals (2021)

In the Wrong Body: Transgender Issues from a Biblical Perspective (2020)

Dangerous Worship: Little Book Series #5 (2020)

The Third Sex? Revisited: Homosexual and Transgender Issues from a Biblical Perspective (2020)

What's So Bad about Hell?: Little Book Series #4 (2019)

Islamic Studies (2nd ed.): Equipping the Christian Witness to Muslims (2019)

Spiritual Health: Little Book Series #3 (2018)

The Preposterous God: The Little Book Series #2 (2018)

Biblical Christianity is Evangelical: Little Book Series #1 (2018)

If Allah Wills (2018) (Arabic Edition, 2018)

False Prophets Among Us: What Is the New Apostolic Reformation and Why Is It Dangerous? (2017)

If God Wills: Bringing the Crescent to the Cross (2016)

Memoirs of a Jesus Freak (2nd Ed.) (2016)

Christian Basics: Lessons, Debates, and Conversations (2015)

Why I Am a Christian, Vol. 2 (2014)

The Soul Journey: How Shamanism, Santería, Wicca and Charisma Are Connected (2014)

Deliver Us from Evil: How Jesus Casts Out Demons Today (2014)

A Matter of Life and Death: Understanding True and False Conversion (2014)*

If the Devil Wrote a Bible (2013)

Awakenings in America and the Jesus People Movement (2011)

How to Care for Your Pastor: A Guide for Small Churches (2007)

Are You Really Born Again? Understanding True and False Conversion (2005) republished and edited as *above

Are You Being Duped? (2004)

Why I Am a Christian (2002)

For Pastors of Small Churches (2001)